THE RIGHT VIEW

THE RIGHT VIEW

Jonathan D Robinson

ATHENA PRESS
LONDON

THE RIGHT VIEW
Copyright © Jonathan D Robinson 2006

All Rights Reserved

No part of this book may be reproduced in any form
by photocopying or by any electronic or mechanical means,
including information storage and retrieval systems,
without permission in writing from both the copyright
owner and the publisher of this book.

ISBN 1 84401 725 7

First Published 2006 by
ATHENA PRESS
Queen's House, 2 Holly Road
Twickenham TW1 4EG
United Kingdom

Printed for Athena Press

*This book is dedicated to
Margaret Thatcher, who defeated socialism
and to Chrissie Yates, who inspired me to write.*

Contents

Introduction   9

1   Socialism   11
     The Third Way   12
     Capitalism   14
     The Insurance of Property   15
     Everything Through Economics   16
     Freedom   17
     The Rule of Law   18
     Conclusions   19

2   State Television?   21
     Crime   22
     Education   24
     The Post Office   26
     Conclusions   27

3   The European Union   29
     The Common Agricultural Policy   29
     The Euro   31
     The United States of Europe   33
     The EU Army   37
     What the EU should be
     and what we can do about it   38
     Conclusions   41

4   God Bless America   44
     Free-enterprise Capitalism and the Third World   45

Nuclear Weapons 47

Terrorism 51

Conclusions 52

5 Rogue States 55

Introduction 55

The Iraqi Victory 55

Libya 58

North Korea 61

Iran 66

In Our Interests 73

Conclusions 75

6 Dealing With Potential Rogue States 79

Introduction 79

Rogues of the Future 79

The Holy Land 83

Zimbabwe 91

Conclusions 99

7 The Fall of Communism 103

Introduction 103

Vietnam 104

Cuba 107

China 111

Conclusions 113

Postscript 117

Select Bibliography and Further Reading 119

Introduction

All my life, all seventeen and a bit years of it, I have been aware of what I should believe. Growing up in the former mining town of Barnsley, the capital of the People's Republic of South Yorkshire, I have been surrounded by socialist sentiment, Marxist ideologies and, above all, a hatred of the Conservative Party, not to mention of Margaret Thatcher. Yet, for as long as I can remember, I have been a Conservative. My parents have had absolutely no influence on this whatsoever, both of them never saying what they believed to be the right view. Despite this, I always had the feeling that there was 'something' in Barnsley against the party that I supported. It was not until relatively recently that I discovered that this 'something' was the 1984–1985 miners' strike and the subsequent pit closures. I sympathise with the miners and their families, for I too have experienced what redundancy can do, as my father was made redundant after over twenty-seven years' services with Barnsley Council – please note, a Labour council.

Despite the feeling towards my party in my home town, I have always felt that the Conservative way was the right way for me. I have never been inclined to follow the popular left-wing, anti-Conservative, anti-Thatcher views of the majority in Barnsley, despite seeing some of those in my own generation being swallowed up by it. I was never inclined to follow, to be 'one of the crowd' – I believe that people should follow their own beliefs and instincts, not the correct or popular view. Indeed, it was this very rejection of consensus that made me first support and then join the Conservative Party. My Conservative membership and my Thatcherite views no doubt make me a traitor in the eyes of some of those in my home town. But, if a traitor is somebody who stands up for freedom because their beliefs and opinions are against the popular consensus, then I am a traitor.

It was these very beliefs, or, if you like, my treachery, that made me write this book. In *The Right View* I first of all set out my basic beliefs and the theories behind them and then I go on to apply them on first a national, then a European, and finally a global scale. All the opinions in this book are my own and no one else's, even if the views I express in this book are the same as those expressed by other people – including political parties. To those who say: 'What does he know?' or 'He should keep his nose out', I have a simple answer. Firstly, there is nobody in the world who knows the opinions expressed in this book better than I do for, as I have already said, they are all my own opinions. Secondly, I not only believe that everybody should have an opinion but I also believe that it is pointless to have an opinion if you don't express it. In addition to this, by telling somebody to 'keep their nose out' you are denying them the right to free speech and therefore their freedom, the most important right of all. Indeed, that is the very reason for writing this book, my belief in freedom for all.

Chapter 1
SOCIALISM

Socialism may, to many people, seem to be a thing of the past, an idea that passed away as the Soviet Union fell. But this is not the case. Socialism is here today, albeit with a suitably spun name. Socialism today may not seem as extreme as it once did but the inherent problems of socialism still remain. Therefore it is essential that we never forget what old socialism stood for and what it can lead to.

Socialism of the old creed, the 'second way' as it became known, stood for equality through the redistribution of wealth through state control of industry and resources. Socialism is often run by one person's ideas, which of course leads to progress in the areas that the one person who is in charge decides are important, which in turn leads to a lack of progress in other areas. Such actions can have terrible consequences. The best example of this was when Mao Tse-tung decided to concentrate all China's workforce on the production of steel in an expansion attempt known as the 'Great Leap Forward'. As the workforce produced steel, agriculture was neglected and in the following years a famine, in which millions of people died, ensued. This is a chilling reminder of what happens when one person decides what is best for an entire people.

The other common result of this kind of socialism, arguably the worst result, is a reduction of the freedom of individuals. As a socialist government takes control of industry and property, people are increasingly put at the mercy of the government. The most powerful expression of what can result, comes not from the right but from a key communist figure. In 1937 Leon Trotsky said of the socialist state:

In a country where the sole employer is the state, opposition means death by slow starvation. The old principle: who does not work shall not eat has been replaced by a new one: who does not obey shall not eat.[1]

This, it must be remembered, came from a man who one would expect to be extolling the virtues of socialism. Indeed, Trotsky may have thought of such blatant oppression of people's freedom as being a desirable thing. When dealing with socialism, in whatever form, in whatever guise, this past, the roots from which socialism comes, must be remembered.

It seems obvious that socialism, given the right conditions, can progress into communism. As socialism is, by definition, a left-wing political ideology, it may seem strange to say that it can lead to fascism, which is on the extreme right of politics. However, it is not so strange when one remembers that the Nazi party, the biggest fascist party ever, stands for the National Socialist Party. Many socialists will argue that socialism and National Socialism are completely different. This is proved wrong as, in 1941, Adolf Hitler said: 'Basically National Socialism [Nazism] and Marxism [socialism] are the same.'[2]

So, despite what socialists may claim, socialism can lead to fascism, just as it can lead to communism. Of course, when fully developed, socialism (communism) and National Socialism (Nazism) are equal in their evil, oppressive, totalitarian ways.[3]

The Third Way

Today socialism is presented to us not as socialism but under various politically correct names. Indeed, it seems that socialists spend the majority of their time thinking up new names for what are, essentially, the same old socialist ideas. After 'socialism' became discredited, 'social democracy', a brand of Marxism, became popular. 'Social democracy' was soon replaced by 'democratic socialism' (which is the way the New Labour Party

---

[1] Quoted in F. A. Hayek, *The Road to Serfdom*, Chicago, University of Chicago Press, 1994.

[2] Quoted in Ibid.

[3] Socialism and its consequences are discussed in far more detail in F. A. Hayek's *The Road to Serfdom*.

describes itself). Now, the latest left-wing way of describing 'modern' socialism is the 'third way'. Those on the left would have us believe that the third way is a glorious middle ground between capitalism and socialism. However, a better description would be a desolate no-man's land of nonsensical ideas. Indeed, the third way is so socialist it hardly deserves its own 'way' at all.

Proponents of the third way would have us believe that it is a way of 'taming' capitalism, a way of allowing industry to flourish whilst providing an advanced welfare state system. This goal, however well intentioned, is unachievable. Despite the fact the welfare state appears to be an attractive proposal, an over-advanced welfare state leads to people relying on the state, which can, of course, lead to a state that controls the actions of its citizens. Additionally, even though an over-advanced welfare state is in itself an undesirable thing, an advanced welfare state is rarely compatible with an economic environment conducive to capitalist competition. The taxes required to pay for an over-advanced welfare state are so high that industrial growth is discouraged as any wealth produced is immediately removed by the state. But in order to see the full consequences of the third way we must look at what the third way has caused in practice.

The best example of the third way in practice is the Blair government. According to Mr Blair, his government would ensure good public services and good standards of living through his system of 'tax credits' – his 'New Deal'. At the same time he said that he would ensure that business could flourish and develop without undue hindrance from the state. Indeed, these promises conform to the definition of the third way, but as the Blair government has progressed, the third way has collapsed. The Blair government, instead of allowing industry to flourish, has restricted it with its policy of taxation. The welfare state has become over-complex and this has led to a reliance on state benefits.

The Blair government has, it is clear, reverted to old Labour ways. In its nine years, the Blair government has presided over sixty-six tax rises – which is contrary to its manifesto promise. This government has massively increased council tax rates, which of course deters people from buying their own homes. His government has raised National Insurance contributions (NICs) to such a level that companies have had to lay workers off as a direct result, and this government has introduced a £5 billion a year tax on pension funds.

These are clearly not the actions of a government committed to capitalism and free enterprise. These actions, especially those that affect industry, are extremely dangerous given their tendency to lead to higher and higher state controls as taxes rise. The third way really is yet another name for socialism. What is clear (which is a rare thing when dealing with socialism) is that however many names socialism goes under, however many times it 'reinvents' itself, it will always be the same old socialism.

Capitalism

As socialism is so clearly a political ideal, which leads only to a state where people's freedoms are removed, and no progress can be made, it is clear that capitalism is the only way that allows individuals the freedom and industry to make progress in areas of their choosing. Capitalism is the 'first way', however none other than Karl Marx, the inventor of the 'second way', first coined the word 'capitalism'. Capitalism's aims are to allow industry, not the state, to decide how resources should be used and where gains from any advances made should go. Capitalism also promotes individual ownership of property, which acts as an insurance against oppressive governments.[4]

Even though capitalism has made the world we live in how it is, there are some people who denounce it as the greatest evil the world has. These people, the anti-capitalists, are a mixture of people ranging from those longing for a return to the old 'glory days' of socialism, to those who believe that capitalism is responsible for poverty in the Third World. Whatever these people's backgrounds, they all share the same goal: to end capitalism and then to redistribute wealth according to some socialist ideal. These anti-capitalists believe that if the world was rid of capitalism, and the wealth and resources in it were equally distributed, then all the world's problems, from poverty to global warming, would be eradicated.

---

[4] The insurance of property ownership is discussed on p.15.

These ideas are pure fantasy. The notion that the limitation of industry through socialism would lead to a reduction in global warming is ludicrous, as industry develops new working practices, which allow more environmentally friendly production methods to be developed. To limit industry would be to reduce prosperity, and it must be remembered that although prosperity may bring environmental problems, it also allows solutions for them. The main grievance of the anti-capitalists, however, is not the environment but poverty in the Third World. The main argument on poverty in the Third World is that the 'West' (i.e. wealthy capitalist nations) exploits the Third World for its own gain. This idea is dispelled by the simple fact that those Third World nations that have the most contact with the West are the best off, whilst those with the least contact with the West are the worst off.[5]

Even though some of the ideas of the anti-capitalists are clearly misguided, they still pose a real threat to capitalism. The idea that money is some form of evil, if it gained support from a large socialists or neo-socialist party, could lead to huge damage being done to capitalism and therefore to the very society in which we live. Such ideas could, if put into practice, lead to the removal of individual rights and freedoms. That is why it is the duty of Conservatives and all other freedom-loving people everywhere to be on their guard against not only socialism – in all its old and modern guises – but also against anti-capitalism (indeed, anti-capitalism is a form of socialism) as both pose a real threat to the world within which we live. It must be remembered that, in the words of Margaret Thatcher in *Statecraft*, 'Money is morally neutral – it's what you do with it that counts.' The forgetting of this point is what allows anti-capitalism to gain such credibility. This is why, therefore, the point must never be forgotten.

The Insurance of Property

Capitalism and conservatism are generally associated with the ownership of property. The Conservative governments from 1979 to 1997 were responsible for the selling of many council houses

---

[5] The issues of the Third World are dealt with in Chapter 4.

nationwide. Why was this? Why are capitalism and conservatism so widely associated with property ownership? The reason is simple: private property is a defence against a would-be totalitarian government. The owners of property are much less likely to be held to ransom by a government trying to rule over all aspects of life. Indeed, the tradition of property ownership in Britain may be one of the reasons why socialism was never able to fully take hold in this country.

Property guards against a government which may try to intimidate its citizens, as it is difficult to evict people from private property, short of using force, which would probably provoke an adverse reaction from the international community or indeed the other citizens of that country. Where property is rented – especially from the state – it is easy to evict someone without drawing particular attention to the fact that the action was politically motivated. This method of using the threat of eviction to force people to obey has been used in many countries – especially communist ones. Even though property does insure us against governments that might try to remove our freedom by more covert means (in a way which would attract as little international attention as possible), it does not protect us against governments that would oppress us by overt means. This is why when a government starts to oppress its people – by whatever means – it is the duty of the international community to stop the government by all possible methods.[6]

Everything Through Economics

It may seem that so far all arguments relating to freedom and individual happiness are somehow related to economics. Indeed, it is true that the majority of arguments relating to freedom have to do with economics. That is why many socialists argue that their control would only be over economic matters and would set people free and would allow them to pursue 'higher values'. The idea that economics is a thing that is separate from all other aspects of life is incorrect. Economics affect how much people are paid, what they can buy and what they can do, so therefore

---

[6] The issue of oppressive foreign governments is dealt with in Chapter 5.

whoever controls the economy also controls the people. That is why, to ensure individuals' freedom, the state must play a minimal role in the running of the economy (in other words the economy must not be consciously directed).

It may seem strange to say that if the state controls industry, then the people of that country have their freedoms reduced. But, however strange it might sound, that is the case for when the state takes control of industry, not only does it effectively control the economy (which means that the state becomes the sole employer – an eerie throwback to that comment made in 1937 by Leon Trotsky[7]), but it also limits people's freedoms in another, less direct way. As the state (or indeed the highest ranking government figure) decides what industry needs to use resources on, other areas of industry are neglected. This not only leads to backwardness in 'unimportant' areas, but it also leads to a reduction in individual choice and therefore a reduction in individual freedom.

It is true that economics plays a part in almost all aspects of our lives, despite what the Left might say to the contrary. That is why, therefore, control over the economy means a control over individuals and the repression of their freedoms. In addition the state can remove freedoms through the limitation of what industry can use its resources on. That is why whenever the argument, 'It's only economics' is used, we must view whoever said it with great mistrust.

Freedom

Freedom is the right that must always be preserved. But what is freedom? The idea of freedom being where individuals can do as they choose and when they choose would find very little support outside anarchist circles. Complete freedom from all restrictions is impossible – this would of course lead to a state where some members of society would harm others. Freedom, therefore, must be the line between anarchy and the police state. Freedom not only affects the individual, it also affects industry, and therefore the economy. Economic freedom must be available if industry is to progress and therefore for individual freedom to be retained.

---

[7] See p.11.

When the economy is consciously directed, areas of industry are often neglected, which leads to a reduction of choice and therefore a reduction in individual freedom. It is true that choice means freedom. The more choice we have, the greater the freedom we have. This applies to everything from jobs to brands of tea. With developments in industry, our choice increases and therefore our freedom also increases. That is why we must be on our guard against economic regulations and controls that limit industry, as they also limit our freedom. The only time that the state should limit our freedom is when an action taken by an individual would cause harm to or reduce the freedom of another individual. Then the state should only make these limitations through the rule of law.

The Rule of Law

The rule of law is the most powerful and most important safeguard that we have. The rule of law is the idea that law is the supreme instrument that governs the actions of individuals and the actions of the state itself. It embodies the principle that an individual can only be punished if they have committed an act that is contrary to pre-defined law. The rule of law also incorporates the idea that justice should be blind and that people should be punished equally for the same offences. The application of the rule of law is dealt with in the next chapter.

The rule of law is the only way freedom can be properly maintained. It is imperative that nobody should be above the law – being so is especially dangerous if the person who is exempt from the law is the head of government.[8] When an individual is above the law they (especially in official office) can then effectively do as they please and, in certain circumstances, even make rules to suit themselves. This is what happened in Germany when the 'Enabling Act' gave Hitler the right to make laws as he saw fit and made him above all authority. If nobody is above the law, which is one of the key principles of the rule of law, then the law gives people their best defence against an oppressive government. The rule of law stops

---

[8] That is not to say that sovereign immunity should not exist. This matter is discussed in detail in Thatcher's *Statecraft*.

the oppression of people's freedom as long as there is an independent judiciary to enforce laws that exist to protect people's freedom. The other way the rule of law protects freedom is that it allows people to have knowledge of laws that protect their freedom, which gives them a great defence. The greatest protector of individual freedom is individual thought and knowledge.

Conclusions

- We must remember that socialism is alive today – albeit under a different name.

- We must remember what socialism stems from and what it can lead to.

- The third way is non-existent. It is just another form of socialism – and a weak one at that.

- An over-advanced welfare state does more harm than good and is rarely, if ever, conducive to capitalism.

- The third way, in action under Tony Blair, is just a reinvention of socialism.

- Conservatives everywhere must take pride in the fact that we have changed very little. Mr Blair's cries of, 'The same old policies, the same old party, the same old Tories!' extols the fact that we Conservatives don't have to change our policies constantly like Labour, as we have policies that work.

- Capitalism is the only way to preserve freedom and to advance and increase freedom.

- Capitalism does not need taming, it should be allowed to progress freely – only laws to prevent fraud and to protect consumers (etc.) are required.

- As the old days of socialism have passed away, we should remember that socialism still exists – the most militant and dangerous modern socialists are the anti-capitalists.

- Anti-capitalists believe capitalism is responsible for almost all ills in the world – this notion is pure fantasy.

- If anti-capitalism took hold, our freedoms would be removed.

- As Margaret Thatcher put it: 'Money is morally neutral – it's what you do with it that counts.'

- Privately-owned property is an excellent defence against a government trying to remove freedom by covert means.

- Property is no defence against overt means of oppression. Therefore the international community must stop the seizure of private property and any other means of oppression.

- Economics and freedom are inextricably linked.

- If the economy is consciously directed, whoever controls the economy controls the people.

- Direction of the economy leads to a reduction of choice and therefore freedom.

- The argument of 'It's only economics' must be viewed with great mistrust.

- Freedom must be preserved at all costs.

- Freedom should mean that individuals can do as they choose, when they choose, provided that their actions will not harm or restrict another's freedom.

- The more choice we have, the freer we are.

- The rule of law is the most powerful defence we have against oppression.

- Under the rule of law, justice should be blind.

- Nobody should be above the law.

- An independent judiciary is the only way of maintaining freedom.

- Public knowledge of laws is the greatest defender of freedom.

Chapter 2

STATE TELEVISION?

Today we live in a world where people demand the 'right to know', and they have an excellent choice of where they get their information. The numerous television stations offer the latest news twenty-four hours a day and the Internet allows information to be obtained almost instantly from a huge variety of politically non-aligned sources. But despite all this choice the best-known and probably most used news service is the BBC. The BBC receives over £2.5 billion of public money every year. So, in this capacity as the main public broadcaster, you would expect the BBC to be completely neutral and to give an objective and unbiased coverage of current affairs. However, this is far from the truth. So is the BBC British 'state television'? Is it the mouthpiece of the government, constantly sending forth pro-government propaganda? Again, these ideas are untrue. But one thing is certain: the BBC is far from being politically unbiased.

The BBC would claim that as both the major political parties are unhappy with its coverage then it must be doing a reasonable job. This is not the case. One only has to watch the political coverage by the BBC to realise that it is instinctively leftward-leaning. The tone of questions put to Conservative politicians and the general tone of its reporting show that the BBC is far from politically unbiased. What is even more insidious than this are the anti-Conservative and leftward messages constantly being put across in the BBC's drama and comedy programmes. Of course, this 'leftwardness' should cause little surprise. Gavyn Davies, the BBC's former chairman and Greg Dyke, the BBC's former director-general, are both known to have been major financial supporters of the Labour Party. Are these really the type of people who should be running a state-funded, supposedly unbiased media company?

At allegations of bias, the BBC's directors always call for specific examples of bias. So, in answer to these calls, I present the BBC's coverage of the 2003 local elections. The programme clearly assumed that the Conservative Party would perform badly. This assumption was not made on any evidence but on what Rod Liddle, former editor of *Today*, described as: 'a predisposition against the Conservative Party'.[9] The Conservative Party presented information about this to the BBC and the BBC admitted that the Conservative Party had a 'right to complain'.[10] So, by the BBC's own admission, they do have a 'predisposition' against the Conservative Party and therefore they have a political bias to the left.

The presenting of such information brings us on to another matter: the fact that the BBC is only answerable to itself. All complaints about the BBC's bias (and all other complaints for that matter) are dealt with by the BBC without any independent control. The BBC is one of the few companies where its governors (who are always the first to defend it from attack) are its highest regulators. The set-up of the BBC has strong similarities with the government of the USSR; they are both answerable to no one. It is true to say that the BBC is not state TV – socialist TV would be closer to the mark.

Crime

Crime has a tendency to make the news – though not always in a direct form. As well as reports of crimes, the issue of crime and what should be done about it appears in the headlines from various sources, be it reports from think tanks or policy pledges from the political parties. Crime always seems to get a lot of attention from politicians, who pledge anything, from more police to tougher sentences, to more community punishment orders. The latter seems to have been in favour in the last few years (in favour by the Labour Party at least). But we must ask ourselves whether community punishment works. Should 'softer' sentences be used, and, if not, what are the alternatives?

---

[9] Quoted in *Heartland Magazine*, October 2003.
[10] Ibid.

Community punishments are a popular sentencing option for a variety of crimes. The idea behind these 'punishments' is that offenders should repay the damage they have done to society. However the idea that picking up litter or tidying graveyards would deter offenders from reoffending or offending in the first place quite simply beggars belief. Such 'soft sentences' are hardly something that the would-be offender would be afraid of. The only thing that would really make the potential criminal think again is the threat of the loss of liberty. This is not to say that all offences serious enough to go before a court warrant a custodial sentence. I fully support the idea of electronically 'tagging' criminals where the authorities can track a criminal's whereabouts, as this not only means that curfew orders can be enforced, but also means that the sense of freedom and privacy is reduced – something most people do not relish the thought of. In addition to this, for offences that do not warrant a custodial sentence, the best idea is to hit the offender where it hurts the most – the pocket.

Despite such measures, it is clear that in some cases prison is the only option. It is often said that prison only acts as an 'academy of crime' where offenders go in, learn the 'trade secrets' of crime and go on to commit more serious offences. This no doubt goes on, but rather than being an argument against custodial sentences, it goes to show that first-time offenders and low-level criminals should not be housed in the same prisons as repeat offenders and more 'hardened' criminals. This segregation of prisoners should go on alongside the current security classification of prisoners, so that prisoners have little opportunity to mix with other prisoners who may lead them in to higher-level crime.

Having said this, however, there is little point in simply throwing somebody in prison. Without rehabilitation, prisoners are likely to reoffend, so an effective rehabilitation scheme is vital. A good example of rehabilitation of prisoners is a scheme run in Texas, USA. Under this scheme, prisoners with about two years of their sentences left to serve can apply to join a religious education programme. The prisoners who go on this programme are not forced to do so nor do they receive any special privileges. This scheme has helped to dramatically cut the crime rate in

Texas. There is, therefore, no reason why similar schemes should not work in the UK. Such schemes may include religious education, but could also include training for specific trades or professions. Such schemes would give prisons a whole new association with the word 'academy'.

When dealing with criminals we must remember that the only way to stop reoffending and to deter people from offending in the first place is to use punishments that they (criminals and would-be criminals) would be afraid of. One of the weaker arguments against such measures (i.e. custodial sentences) is that such punishments lead to the general, law-abiding public becoming afraid of the state. The answer to this is quite simple: if people have committed no crime then they have nothing to be afraid of. As I have said earlier, freedom is the most important thing in the world; only the threat of its denial (that is, of course, in accordance with the rule of law[11]) will stop people breaking the law.

Education

Education in this country has changed greatly since earlier days. The days of the eleven-plus have been surpassed by SATs and ALS interventions. But has education evolved too far? Are all the targets and bureaucracy necessary? In many cases the 'evolution' has gone too far, in that the constant desire to achieve targets has become overriding. In the time I was in school (1993–2005) I saw teaching methods become more and more government-dictated and target-driven. Education has, in recent years, become obsessed with targets and league tables, to such an extent that the only things that seem to matter are averages.

It seems quite incredible to me that in primary schools, children aged around eight years, who have been identified as underachieving in English, are placed on 'intervention schemes', which, instead of teaching the basics, teach them new terminology that is not normally taught. These 'intervention schemes' that are supposed to bring underachievers up to that all-important 'average' mark, have no real bearing on the subject they are supposed to assist in. Surely a better way would be for one to one

---

[11] See p.18.

assistance from the class teacher to be given. The argument against this is that teachers do not have enough time, but surely time could be made if the amount of wasteful paperwork (i.e. the huge amount of long-term lesson planning) that teachers have to complete was reduced.

There has been a tendency in education at all levels to focus on only academic qualifications. This is a tendency best represented by the Blair government's target that 50 per cent of school leavers go to university by a certain date. This desire to increase the number of graduates has lead to degrees such as 'Golf Club Management' and even 'David Beckham Studies' appearing at some universities. Such degrees cheapen qualifications and therefore damage the entire British educational system. What must be accepted is that not all people are academic and therefore not all people are suited to gaining academic qualifications. Instead of introducing more 'academic' qualifications in what are traditionally vocational subject areas, so as to achieve unrealistic targets, it would surely be a better idea to introduce more vocational qualifications – a measure which would surely help to alleviate the dearth of vocationally skilled workers.

It is clearly important that key subjects such as English and maths should be taught to all to a certain level. However, beyond this basic level, there seems to me to be very little point in teaching a subject to all, when it is clear that to some the subject will have no relevance whatsoever or that they have no ability in that subject. Rather than the 'one size fits all' system, it would be better to tailor lessons to individual strengths. This would allow individuals to progress further in life, as they would know more about a subject that they are interested and talented in. Therefore all students must be given greater choice in what they study. Such action would lead to more people being skilled in different areas, rather than several state-determined areas.

For our education system to progress, therefore, it needs to become less obsessed with the meeting of targets and quotas. In education there needs to be more of an emphasis on the talents of individuals. This means that in addition to the current academic education system, there needs to be more vocational skills taught – especially in secondary and further education. But such vocational education and training must not be given across the board; those who are 'academic' must be educated academically whilst those who are 'vocational' must be taught vocationally. Remember, it would be pointless to teach algebra to a plumber just as it would be pointless to teach soldering to a mathematician. The idea that this leads to an unequal education system is wrong; this system would educate individuals according to individual needs, in areas that they are more likely to use later in life. The key point that must be remembered is that education is not there to do the best for targets and quotas, but to do the best for those who are being educated.

The Post Office

A popular way to study these days is via correspondence course. The only problem with this is not the course, but its delivery method: the post. Of all the services in this country, the day to day sending of mail is the most archaic. Royal Mail is a single company with effective control over an entire market – in other words a monopoly; is this really the right way for a modern day country, which is supposed to stand for the ideas of free enterprise and competition? As the general post system is neither free nor enterprising, the answer to this question is no, it is not right for one single organisation to have complete control over one whole market.

As I have pointed out earlier, choice is freedom; therefore a denial of choice is a denial of freedom. It may sound rather extreme to say that only having one company to deliver general mail is a denial of freedom, but only having one company to deliver the mail means that it can charge whatever it wants without the fear of losing custom. Therefore, how much we pay for post is in the hands of a company with nothing to lose and only money to gain. But, what must be the biggest complaint against the postal system is that it rides roughshod over the principle that everybody should have the right to freedom of choice and that individuals should get value through free capitalist competition. It may seem an almost petty matter but the fact that competition does not exist where it could do well for the public is abhorrent. Indeed, the only time when competition alone should not provide a service is when it cannot or where it could lead to damage being done to individuals (i.e. the health service).

The postal service must open up to competition as parcel delivery services have done. This would not only provide more choice and therefore more freedom to individuals, it would also help to keep seemingly ever-increasing postal prices down. The argument against opening the postal service up to competition is the logistics required to do so. People ask: 'How would different companies collect post?' and 'How would people pay?' There are, of course, several ways in which this could be done. However, there can be no doubt that the entrepreneurs, who have helped make this nation what it is today, would find an innovative solution to the problem.

Conclusions

- Whatever it might claim, the BBC is often biased in its coverage of the news – the tone of its questions and reports shows that.

- The BBC is instinctively anti-Conservative in everything from the news to its comedy.

- The BBC should be run by people who support no political party.

- The BBC should have an independent body to deal with complaints against it – its governors should not be its highest regulators.

- The fact that community punishments are popular does not make them an effective deterrent against crime.

- The only way to stop reoffending and offending in the first place is to use punishments that the offenders and the would-be offender would be afraid of.

- The loss of liberty is the only real deterrent against crime.

- Electronic 'tagging' is an excellent way of deterring crime.

- Whatever other sentencing options there are, prison will sometimes be the only option.

- Prisoners should be imprisoned with those who have committed similar levels of crime to them; it is most important to stop prisons becoming 'academies of crime'. This can be achieved by not housing repeat and first-time offenders together.

- Prison alone does not work; rehabilitation, which allows prisoners to get out of the crime cycle, makes prison work.

- Education has become too obsessed with targets; it needs to focus more upon the individual.

- There is no point in making traditionally vocational qualifications into academic qualifications just to fulfil targets and quotas; such actions are damaging to the whole education system.

- Vocational skills are just as valuable as academic skills; individuals should be taught according to their individual talents.

- The postal system, as it presently is, blatantly flouts our right to freedom of choice.

- The lack of competition in the postal market means that Royal Mail can charge whatever it wants, without much risk of losing custom.

- To ensure that the principle of freedom of choice is upheld and that people receive the best value for money, the general postal market must open up to competition.

- Whatever the logistical problems of such action, we must not doubt that the great minds of British business will come up with a suitable answer.

Chapter 3

THE EUROPEAN UNION

For any of the ideas in the last chapter to be implemented, there is one thing that must be present – Britain's right to rule herself. But an institution that was supposed to help us is slowly taking this right to self-rule away. The greatest threat to our sovereignty today is not some hostile foreign force, but the European Union (EU). The EU is damaging our economy and endangering our right to self-rule with its continuous interference into the running of this country. The EU is becoming more than a union of countries with economics links; it is becoming a superstate. In this chapter, I aim to show what damage the EU is doing to us, what it is on the verge of doing and what we can do about it.

The Common Agricultural Policy

The Common Agricultural Policy (CAP), like socialism, is a thing commonly associated with the past. Like socialism, the CAP lingers on. The original idea behind the CAP was, in post-war Europe, to protect against food shortages by providing farmers with a fixed price for all the food they produced. This idea certainly worked; in fact it worked too well. This policy led to so-called food 'mountains' and 'lakes' being formed. The CAP was then limited so that farmers were only paid subsidies on a certain amount of produce, which kept the cost of the CAP down. This action led to one of the most incredible happenings of recent years: farmers being encouraged to reduce production – in fact being paid to do so. Such actions may seem crazy when some countries are short of food, but when you consider that the bureaucrats of the EU put these measures in place, it is hardly surprising.

The idea of the CAP is so outdated, so unnecessary in today's world – yet nobody even attempts to justify it. But this is hardly surprising; to try to justify the CAP would be to try to justify the unjustifiable. The CAP now costs the EU taxpayer £30 billion a year – around half of the EU's total budget. Not only does the CAP impose a huge tax burden, it also means that food prices for EU consumers are pushed up. But, just so non-EU countries don't feel left out, the CAP also depresses worldwide food prices, which deprives farmers in poorer countries of their living. The CAP does so by damaging free trade, which is the only thing that can help poorer countries.

The CAP causes EU protectionism. This protectionism – in other words the EU intervening in the economy – greatly damages not only our economy but also the world economy. The CAP costs the EU an estimated \$50 billion a year in higher prices, inefficient production methods and economic distortions – not to mention the actual cost to taxpayers. This means that because of the CAP and other forms of EU protectionism, we are forced to pay over the odds for goods, which is a blatant violation of our freedom of choice. The CAP costs the rest of the world \$25 billion a year in lost export opportunities, which causes great damage to developing nations as they rely heavily on their agricultural sectors. The CAP is the world's largest protectionist force and the most damaging to developing nations. Something all the EU socialists might like to think about is the fact that their protectionist intervention in the world economy – a typical socialist trait – causes huge damage to poorer nations. And they still have the cheek to claim that free-enterprise capitalism is the greatest, most damaging evil in the world.

The CAP, therefore, is one of the most damaging economic forces in the world today. Its protectionism not only affects consumers in the EU, it also affects people worldwide. Greatest affected are countries which rely heavily upon agriculture. Inside the EU, consumers are forced to pay higher food prices than the rest of the world. This system clearly damages our freedom of choice and therefore freedom itself. Obviously the CAP cannot be removed overnight as the effect on European agriculture would be disastrous. The only real solution to the problems caused by the CAP is to remove it over a number of years. Of course, such a method would still affect agriculture if other current EU measures such as import tariffs remained in place. But if there was truly global free enterprise, then the removal of the CAP would benefit not only poorer countries and EU consumers, but also EU farmers, as, without the negative effect of the CAP, they would have free access to much larger markets than before.

The Euro

By far the most talked about issue raised by the EU is the single currency – the euro. According to proponents of the euro, it has been designed for purely economic reasons. But, there are of course, other reasons – the main one being the creation of a European superstate. The desire to create such a state is an old one, stretching back several centuries. The best description of the link between a single currency and a superstate comes not from a modern EU bureaucrat but from Napoleon Bonaparte. He said:

> A monetary identity throughout Europe along with a common legal system would have achieved a single family in Europe. No one would ever have left home while travelling.[12]

Such a statement could have come from any of the modern pro-euro thinkers. It shows imperialistic intent – especially when you remember where it came from. Napoleon Bonaparte was clearly calling for some form of European superstate. It must be remembered that individual nations, under such a 'unified' system, would have lost the right to decide what was best for them. Yet today people call for a Europe with a single monetary identity and unified legal system. If history ever held a warning, this is it.[13]

The fact that the euro was clearly designed to bring more than a single currency to Europe is reason in itself to reject it but, even so, there are very good economic reasons why Britain should not join the single currency. For a start, as I have said earlier, when a state starts to remove the right of individuals to take economic decisions, then individuals lose their freedom. The same applies when a supra-national authority takes over the economy of a nation – that

---

[12] Margaret Thatcher, *Statecraft*, London, HarperCollins, 2003.
[13] The issue of a European superstate is dealt with on p.33.

nation loses the right to govern itself and to decide what is best for its people. The pro-euro lobby denounce such statements as 'nationalistic' or even downright crazy; they use the old argument of, 'It's only economics.' They say, 'How can an economic union lead to the removal of a nation's right to self-government?' Quite simply, as a matter of fact. For, when a nation's economy is controlled by a supra-national authority (controlled in the sense of interest and borrowing rates, etc. rather than in the sense of consciously directed, although this can happen), that supra-national authority can quite easily force a nation state to do something by threatening to damage that nation's economy. A supra-national economic authority can in fact remove the right to self-government in a very similar way that a socialist state can remove individuals' freedom by consciously directing the economy.

One of the main arguments in support of the euro is that it would save money and therefore benefit economies by cutting out the need to change currency when trading with other countries. This idea is fine until you remember that there is a world outside the EU. As 64.5 per cent of British direct investment overseas is outside the EU and just over half the foreign direct investment in Britain comes from outside the EU, the amount saved from exchanging money would not radically alter the British economy. The argument that, given time, the euro would become the world's 'trade currency' is null and void as we already have a global trade currency – it is called the US dollar.

Another economic reason why Britain should not join the euro was first made by one of the EU's earliest architects – Charles de Gaulle. De Gaulle said that Britain should not enter the EU as we were 'different' from the rest of Europe – geographically, historically and economically. This is very true as the rest of Europe relies far more heavily on agriculture and such like, whereas Britain relies on the service sector and other such sectors. This difference shows why Britain should not be part of the euro, because an economic action that might be good for Europe is not necessarily going to be good for Britain. Evidence for this is when Britain joined the European Exchange Rate Mechanism (ERM) in 1987. In this, sterling shadowed the Deutschmark, which led to interest rates being left too low, allowing inflation to rise. This eventually caused

'Black Wednesday' on 16 September 1992. After this, sterling left the ERM and the British economy eventually recovered. If that is what happened to the British economy when we joined the ERM, think what could happen if we joined the euro – but with the euro (unlike the ERM) there could be no going back.

That is the main problem with the euro. Once Britain had abolished the pound in favour of the euro and then found that the grass was not greener on the Euroland side, there could be no going back. If, after adopting the euro, Britain found that measures taken for the good of most of Europe caused harm to the British economy, we would be forced to suffer such measures, as our economy, so very different from the rest of Europe's, would be inextricably linked to the rest of the euro area.

To this, supporters of the euro might argue that for free trade within Europe to be maximised, we need to have the same currency as the rest of Europe, or that we should join the euro to make ourselves closer to the 'heart of Europe', so if there are things that we don't like we can have more 'influence'. The latter, as I shall prove later in this chapter, is a pathetic excuse for an argument. As for the former, there is an excellent example, already in existence, of why the same currency is not necessary for free trade. The North American Free Trade Area (NAFTA), which comprises the USA, Canada and Mexico, is a group that promotes free trade, therefore benefiting the member states without the need for a unified currency, or other unified institutions (i.e. laws or parliaments) for that matter. If such an organisation can benefit economies on the other side of the Atlantic without the need for a single currency, then there is no reason why such an organisation cannot flourish and do good on this side of the Atlantic. After all isn't the EU all about benefiting member states through free trade? If it is, then with NAFTA as an example, there is clearly no need for the euro. But then again, the euro and the EU are clearly about far more than free trade.

The United States of Europe

The euro is clearly aimed at the creation of a European superstate, despite what Mr Blair might say. But, in the EU, there is more than a single currency pushing us towards a European superstate. The ever more meddlesome EU laws that alter standards every other day; the ambiguous European Convention on Human Rights; the European courts upholding these vaguely defined rights; the European Constitution to give the EU the trappings of statehood; the constant desire in the pro-European lobby for ever more unified policies on everything from fisheries to foreign policy and, perhaps most dangerously of all, the desire to set up an EU army – all help the continuous drive for a European super-state. The commissars of the EU would say that all these measures (and doubtless the countless others that exist) are there for the good of the citizens of the EU, and would say that these measures have absolutely nothing to do with a European super-state. But, just as the euro is clearly aimed at more than monetary unification, these measures are clearly aimed at more than the good of the population of the EU.

Before we look at how the EU is trying to create a superstate, we must see why an EU superstate would be so detrimental to us. Apart from the above arguments about the euro and how it could damage our economy, there is the issue of democracy itself. If an EU superstate was formed and a proportional representation system of government was used, such a government would have to make decisions for the good of the largest part of the EU. This largest part of the EU might well not include Britain, which often has different concerns to the rest of Europe. In other words an EU parliament ruling an EU superstate would represent too big an area and therefore would leave some groups (i.e. nations) with their problems unaddressed. It is better to have governments ruling people with similar needs and issues; a supra-national government of Europe would have to represent too many different groups to be effective.

This would be the main problem if an EU superstate existed. There would also be the issue that if a supra-national government ruled the economy, the economic freedom and therefore general freedom of that country would be reduced (and if the superstate government was socialist, then the freedoms of individuals within the member states would also be reduced[14]). This matter is essentially the same as the matter of the euro and is dealt with on page 31.

It is clear that the EU is trying to build a superstate. Indeed, it almost appears that the powers of the EU have listed what is needed to build such a superstate. High on that list would be a single currency and that would be followed by unified laws and a legal system to enforce those laws. The link between currency and state is clear. It is a classic requirement that a state issues its own currency, so when a state ceases to produce its own currency and a supra-national body does this for it, then that state's statehood is clearly diminished. The link between laws and statehood is clear: a state is not a state if it does not make laws. This is so because if a state does not make laws it has no authority or jurisdiction, so therefore it is not a state. So, as the EU's laws cover an increasing amount of areas – from food standards to human rights – individual states' powers to make their own laws is reduced, therefore increasing the power of the EU. Some may argue that this hardly matters, as the EU is simply making laws for the individual states. But, it must be remembered that states contain people with generally similar concerns, so a supra-national authority would make laws to govern too wide a variety of different peoples. In other words, countries are run by governments that know issues on a more local (in the sense of national) level better than a supra-national authority.

The EU's latest superstate-building scheme should come as no surprise whatsoever. As the euro has made a great leap forward in the creation of an EU superstate, it seems logical that the commissars of the EU should take the final step in the building of an EU superstate, that final step being the EU Constitution. Such a constitution would set in stone the EU's already far-reaching and meddlesome powers and give the EU the right to take control of virtually all of our resources (i.e. North Sea oil) and give them even more power to overrule national governments. The issues that an EU constitution raises, such as single EU laws and a single EU foreign policy, are dealt with elsewhere within this chapter

---

[14] See Chapter 1.

but I feel that it is worth mentioning that an EU constitution would effectively be the last block in the building of a European superstate (or moreover the nail in the coffin of the free nation state). A final point as regards the EU Constitution is to those inclined to believe Mr Blair when he says such a constitution would merely be a tidying up exercise. Even Valéry Giscard d'Estaing, one of the main authors of the constitution, disagrees with Mr Blair. Giscard d'Estaing compares himself to the USA's founding fathers, and his work to the US Constitution, though Blairites can make of that what they will.

As a state must have policies covering matters outside its own borders, so the EU has decided that the EU needs a unified foreign policy. This is yet another attempt to blatantly form a superstate on the part of the EU, quite simply because having a single EU foreign policy takes away individual countries' rights to decide what their stance is on an international issue. Any removal of current national veto rights within the EU (something which is proposed by the EU Constitution) would reduce this right still further. This is detrimental to a nation, for if a supra-national authority decided foreign policies, a country would not be able to take action in a particular area of foreign affairs that especially concerned it. The measure of unified foreign policy within the EU (or perhaps the United States of Europe, as some may wish the EU to be called) is aimed particularly against Britain. This is because Britain has, within Europe, traditionally been the country which has taken most international action, so by limiting our right to make our own foreign policy decisions, the EU would be taking away from Britain what General de Gaulle would have called our power to 'cause trouble'. Having this right taken away from us would damage our world standing and therefore damage us in Britain politically and economically.

In response to this it may be said that surely the EU would take decisions that were for the good of the whole EU and therefore if such circumstances came about (that is, where our foreign policy decisions were made by the EU – in other words, if an EU superstate existed), Britain would not be harmed in the slightest, politically and/or economically.

There are two main problems with such an argument. The

first is that in a superstate that represents at least twenty-five countries, some are bound to benefit from a course of action taken which is different from that taken by the EU. The second is that, as Britain has more links outside the EU than other EU countries, a single foreign policy from the EU could be damaging to Britain, given that Britain has strong links with so many other countries (i.e. the Commonwealth). This is why Britain really must not be party to anything that could lead to an EU superstate. If it did, and Britain lost its world standing and links with the world outside Europe, then the damage to Britain would be great.

The EU Army

The desire within the EU to have a single foreign policy for all the member states has lead to a desire for something else within the EU. That is the creation of a European army – although the EU would much rather it be referred to as the 'European Rapid Reaction Force' (ERRF). In fact, the EU completely denies that setting up the opportunity to 'give the EU the means of playing its role fully on the international stage' something that would require a pool of at least 200,000 troops and 'appropriate air and naval elements'[15] – would constitute the setting up of a European army. I may be mistaken, but to me an army is something that a nation has for self-defence and to 'play its role on the international stage' and is made up of, as well as combat troops, 'appropriate air and naval elements'.[16] Perhaps the EU would like all the armies of the world to be renamed 'rapid reaction forces'.

As it is clear that the EU is trying to set up a European army, we must ask ourselves why. The reason is so that it can move its goal of becoming a single superstate into becoming a superpower. The root of this aim lies not in Europe but in the USA and its hegemony within NATO (North Atlantic Treaty Organisation). The EU believes that it must show itself to be equal to the USA – the reasons for this desire are unclear, though it may stem from a desire on the part of the EU to attempt to limit the US economy

---

[15] 'The Presidency Report on European Security and Defense Policy', quoted in Thatcher, *Statecraft*.

[16] Ibid.

(for reasons perhaps based on some left-wing ideology). But, whatever the reasons behind this desire, the EU feels that it must compete with the USA and therefore NATO. It must be understood how gravely serious such a desire could be. It must be remembered that at best the setting up of a European army would provide an alternative to NATO – at worst it could become a rival to NATO and, if that were to happen, Britain would have to decide which side of the Atlantic she stood with.

Despite the obvious fact that the setting up of another large military organisation – the European army – would undermine the American-led NATO, the EU argues that the setting up of the ERRF would, as well as giving the EU the capacity for autonomous military action, strengthen NATO. This argument is particularly easy to see through. If the EU wanted to strengthen NATO, then member states of the EU would simply have to increase their defence spending or advance their military systems so that they were more in line with US military systems, rather than go through the lengthy process of setting up their own army. It is clear that the European army would be a challenge to the USA and NATO, so therefore Britain should play no further part in this, the EU's most dangerous scheme ever.

What the EU should be and what we can do about it

It is plain to see that the EU's main objective is to achieve political unification within Europe. The desire for this objective to be achieved has come from a variety of factors ranging from historical to modern global issues. Indeed, the true root of the desire for a unified Europe is probably only known to the commissars of the EU. However, given the EU's record even this is doubtful. So, as it is clear that no, or very little, good can come out of the EU in its present form, we must decide ourselves what the EU really should be and what it really should stand for. I believe that the EU should be an organisation that stands for free-enterprise capitalism. From this starting block the EU can then achieve what its countless initiatives have attempted to do (that is as a by-product of further developing the EU superstate) over the years – improve standards of living and benefit the world as a

whole. This idea of having a single strategy to achieve goals –
namely capitalism – may be very frightening to the commissars of
the EU, who are only used to having innumerable schemes
managed by armies of bureaucrats, but the EU should realise that,
as I have tried to show earlier, capitalism is the only way to a freer,
better tomorrow.

With this in mind, Britain must make it clear what it wishes its
part within Europe to be. Britain's main objectives should be:

- Making it clear that we do not want the euro.

- Refusing to play any role in the creation of a European
  army or anything else that undermines NATO.

- Refusing to be party to the EU Constitution or such like.

- Lobbying for an EU that promotes freer trade and enterprise, without interfering into how individual nations
  manage their economies.

But knowing what we want from the EU is not enough. We must
know how to get it. Such a statement may sound bloody-minded
but, when the matter in concern affects our right to freedom of
self-rule, we must act in this manner.

To alter the EU for the better, there are several options open
to us. One of these options is a strange Blairite idea. It is the idea
that if there is something within the EU that we dislike and wish
to change, we should make ourselves closer to the heart of Europe
by accepting more EU policies which would therefore (that is,
according to Mr Blair) give us more influence within the EU.
The idea of saying that we should have more to do with an
organisation with which we disagree and accept more of what
they do (with which we probably disagree) is pure madness. The
idea of doing something you disagree with in order to gain
influence is completely devoid of principle and would (and does)
come from someone whose sole aim was to gain more influence
rather than do what is best for Britain.

As it is clear that this frankly crazy Blairite approach would be
doomed to failure, we must look at other, more sensible options
for achieving our goals within the EU. The first option is the

most favourable. That is the creation of a two-tier or multi-tier EU, where member states would only be party to the aspects of the EU that benefited them or that they wished to be part of. It is true that the system exists to some extent today, with only some of the member states not having joined the euro (although, as far as Britain is concerned, this is something that Mr Blair is trying to change).

But this system needs to go further. Nations should only be party to 'sections' of the EU that benefit them. This, in the long term, would benefit all EU member states. It may be argued that to be part of the EU, a nation may have to be part of something that is not necessarily to its benefit. Such an argument is illogical, as, for a country to be part of something that was not to its benefit, perhaps simply to 'stay in with' the EU, would be pointless and potentially damaging. Indeed for this reason, this argument is rarely advanced by anybody other than those who wish to be part of the EU only to gain 'influence'.

However, given that the EU has become so advanced, it may prove impossible to renegotiate the terms on which Britain could be part of a multi-tier EU. So that leaves only one option open to us – that is, besides going along with the current EU (to wherever it is going) – withdrawal from the EU. This may sound extreme but if the preferable option of being part of a multi-tier EU is closed to us, it is either that or become a mere region of a European superstate. But, before actual withdrawal, Britain could use the threat of its withdrawal (which is a real threat, given the size of Britain's EU contribution) to force the EU to create a multi-tier Europe that was favourable to us. But if Britain were to make this threat, she would have to be prepared to carry it out, as it is very likely that not even the threat of the withdrawal of a member state would stop the EU in its seemingly inexorable drive toward the formation of an EU superstate.

So, if Britain were to withdraw from the EU, what would the consequences for Britain be? What is highly unlikely is that Britain's economy would collapse, as the pro-Europeans predict it would. It is nonsensical to say that if Britain left the EU then the other countries of the EU would close their economies to us, as this would cause as much damage to their economies as it would to ours – the rest of Europe needs Britain far more than we need them. In fact, if Britain were no longer a member of the EU, the British economy could even benefit from it, as business would be more free to trade with more of the world than it is currently able to due to EU import tariffs. Also, outside the EU, Britain would no longer have to contribute to the EU, so, therefore, tax levels would be reduced, encouraging business within Britain to grow. If, after leaving the EU, Britain were to turn itself into a Hong Kong-style haven for industry, then Britain's economy would be able to flourish far better than it could within the present EU. The one thing to remember when dealing with the EU is that there is a world outside it.

Conclusions

- Currently, the main aim of the EU is the formation of a superstate.

- The Common Agricultural Policy is outdated and has got to the point of farce.

- The basis of the euro is not founded on economic unification (which is, itself, very dangerous), but in the desire to create a superstate.

- This would lead to sovereign states no longer having any power over their economies and therefore over the state itself.

- NAFTA proves that free enterprise can flourish without a single currency.

- What is economically good sense for one country does not mean that it is so for another. Britain's experience with the ERM is proof of this.

- If Britain joined the euro there would be no going back.

- Virtually everything the EU does is aimed at the creation of a superstate.

- If a European superstate were formed then the interests of some nations would be overlooked.

- It is the most basic symbol of statehood for a nation to issue laws – if it does not then it ceases to be a state. Therefore when a supra-national authority issues laws, it ceases to be a supra-national authority and it becomes a state – moreover, a superstate.

- An EU constitution would give the EU the trappings of statehood.

- A single foreign policy throughout the EU would damage Britain in particular, given Britain's interests outside Europe are different from the rest of the EU.

- The most dangerous part of the EU's drive towards a superstate is the proposed European Rapid Reaction Force (ERRF) or, in other words, the proposed EU Army.

- The argument that an EU Army would strengthen NATO is rubbish – increasing defence expenditure would achieve that.

- The EU Army would cause serious damage to the American-led NATO. At best ERRF would provide an alternative to NATO; at worst, it could be a rival.

- The EU has gone too far in the areas in which it concerns itself.

- The EU should be an economic union, promoting free trade between states.

- Britain should be clear about what she wishes to be part of in the EU, and even clearer on the areas she does not.

- The Blairite drive for 'influence' within the EU could prove to be disastrous for Britain.

- We should push for a 'multi-tier' Europe, which would be the best option for Britain.

- However, I fear that the EU is too advanced for the implementation of a 'multi-tier' system, so Britain's only other option (that is apart from doing nothing) is to withdraw from the EU.

- Britain must remember that the EU needs us far more than we need them.

- Finally, we must never forget that there is a world outside the EU.

Chapter 4

GOD BLESS AMERICA

The terrorist atrocities of 11 September 2001 show quite clearly the feeling of some people towards the USA. Even in Britain, America's closest ally, there are people who see America as an evil. Indeed, it is true to say that most anti-Americans in this country are on the left of the political spectrum – in other words, many anti-Americans are socialists. Of course, that is not to say that all socialists are anti-American or that all anti-Americans are socialists. But the fact that it is generally the socialist left that are anti-American provides us with one of the main roots of the anti-American feeling held within this country. America is the richest nation on earth and its wealth comes from a long-standing commitment to free-enterprise capitalism – this makes it the ultimate symbol of capitalism and therefore of freedom in the world. Many on the socialist left are against America, as they are opposed to capitalism and are therefore opposed to freedom.[17]

In Britain this anti-American feeling, be it socialist or otherwise in origin, quite simply beggars belief. We, in Britain, like the other people of Western Europe, owe our freedom to the Americans. At least twice in the last century the Americans have saved us from oppression. In the Second World War it was the USA joining the war that saved us from Nazi tyranny. After that, US nuclear weapons were what protected the free world for almost half a century from the threat of Soviet domination. It is true to say that twice (arguably three times, given the First World War, although circumstances were somewhat different) in the last century the greatest threat to our freedom has come from Europe, and twice in the last century salvation has come from across the Atlantic. Given this history, we should be sceptical of the EU, and

---

[17] See Chapter 1.

closer to America instead. But, as well as this strong historical link, there are strong current reasons why we should support America.

Firstly, there is the economic reason. As the world's largest economy, America offers huge opportunities for trade and investment that anti-Americans would have closed to us. British direct investment in the USA for the year-end 1999 amounted to over £185 billion. From this it is clear to see that America offers a huge investment opportunity to us. But the financial benefits of supporting America are not the only ones. America is one of the world's freest economies and has a long-standing commitment to freedom – both economic and individual. Therefore, by supporting America economically, we are supporting freedom and its export worldwide.

This leads us on to the second reason we have for supporting America. America is one of the greatest forces – if not the greatest – for freedom in the world, and because of this, it is the world's most powerful nation. Indeed, it is the only nation that can be described as a hyperpower. America is a hugely powerful force for good and freedom in the world, that is, the non-economic version of freedom. This is one of the main reasons why we should support them. Some would say that this meant that we were just supporting America because it is the world's most powerful nation. This is untrue. We support America because, in today's world, it is the driving force behind freedom and free trade. If it were not for America we would not enjoy the freedoms that we currently have. God bless America.

Free-enterprise Capitalism and the Third World

As freedom is the most important right that we have, we must ensure that everybody, throughout the world, has the opportunity to enjoy this, the most fundamental of all rights. The best way to ensure that people worldwide have freedom is through free-enterprise capitalism. Free-enterprise capitalism is, alongside the rule of law, the only way to ensure and increase individual freedoms. So therefore, by exporting capitalism, far from oppressing people as the socialist left so frequently claim, we are actually exporting freedom. It is really quite simple; the more a country trades, the freer it becomes.

This manner of exporting freedom throughout the world is the best way to break the cycle of poverty and increase freedom in the Third World. By trading with the Third World, not only do we benefit by buying a product or service that we desire, but the country that we trade with also benefits as it gains money from trading. It also helps to forge links between countries, which always benefits future trade. Trading with a poorer economy is far more beneficial to it than just giving regular handouts. Such regular handouts are like an over-advanced welfare state system – they lead to reliance on handouts and make the country that is receiving the handout at the mercy of the 'donor' country. Indeed, it is sometimes necessary to send such aid in the time of some disaster, but, in general terms, the way to reduce poverty in the world is through trade, not aid.

At this point the Left normally starts to rant about how poverty is the fault of capitalism and how socialism would cure it, which, as I have tried to show earlier, is complete nonsense. Another favourite of the Left in response to this is that some Third World nations have no natural resources, so therefore they must be given handouts (which they would then become reliant upon). Well, for a start, all Third World countries – indeed all countries in the world – have at least one natural resource – people. The proof that a country can do well without having many natural resources is Japan. For example, it imports over 99 per cent of its oil, and, despite the fact that its economy was left in ruins after the Second World War, it now has a GDP per capita that is higher than the United Kingdom's. This huge turnaround was only possible through free-enterprise capitalism.

The fact that Japan has turned itself from a country in a state of economic collapse, to one of the world's freest and wealthiest nations, despite having no natural resources, and without having an interfering socialist government, is indisputable evidence that the best thing that we can do for the Third World is to trade with it – not just give it handouts. Indeed, the best thing that we can do for people in the Third World is to export capitalism to them – the very worst thing that we can do is to export socialism to them.

For, if we put in place socialist regimes in the Third World, not only would the freedom of the people there be reduced, but given the present unstable state of many of their economies, progress in these countries would be limited to all but a few important areas (as is the general tendency with a socialist regime[18]). This would mean that economic collapse would be likely at the first challenge, as would the disastrous consequence of any such collapse. The only way that we can truly hope to get the Third World out of poverty is to encourage capitalism there and be, ourselves, willing to trade with the Third World.

Nuclear Weapons

During the dark years of the Cold War, only one thing stood between Soviet oppression and us – nuclear weapons. For almost half a century, nuclear weapons kept the uneasy peace between the West and the Soviet Union. The only thing, during the years of the Cold War, which stopped the Soviets seizing control over all of Europe, was that we had the capacity to unleash the terrible destructive power of the hydrogen bomb. Today, with the threat of communism gone from Europe (but not from the world), our nuclear weapons still act as the ultimate deterrent against any nation that would try to overpower us and they are our final safeguards against terrorist states.[19] Yet, despite their continued role in ensuring that the free world remains free, there are some people who advocate the disarmament of not only our own, but of all the nuclear weapons in the world.

These people claim that nuclear weapons are an instrument of oppression, that they are the ultimate force for evil in the world, even though many of these people also argue that capitalism is the ultimate force for evil in the world. (Note that the nuclear disarmament lobby and the anti-capitalists are very often inextricably intertwined.) It appears that such people can't make up their minds as to what is the 'ultimate force of evil' for surely having two 'ultimate evils' is a contradiction in terms. But, despite the contradiction, the nuclear disarmament lobby, alongside the anti-

---

[18] See Chapter 1.

[19] See Chapter 5.

capitalists, are some of the most vocal and most dangerous groups within modern society. They are not dangerous in the sense of what they do, but in the sense that if the ideas they tout were ever put into widescale practice, the consequences for free society would be dire.

For a start, if we alone were to disarm our nuclear weapons, we would open ourselves up to aggression from nations that were hostile to us. By this it must be understood that it would be extremely unlikely for any such state to be another nuclear state but for it to be an aggressive non-nuclear state. If we did not have our nuclear deterrent, then any such nation would be far more likely to attack us, or our interests, as we would not be capable of responding with the most powerful weapon known to humans.

Secondly, if all nuclear armed nations in the world disarmed, not only would all nations (not just those that had disarmed, but also those that were protected by other nations' 'nuclear umbrellas') face what I have described above, but we would also face a threat from certain states – so-called 'rogue states' – who would exploit the lack of nuclear armament in the world. If anybody seriously thinks that if we disarm all currently existing nuclear weapons, that the threat of nuclear war would simply vanish, then they are either very naïve or very stupid. In fact, if we were to disarm all nuclear weapons in the world, then the threat of a nuclear strike on us would actually grow rather than vanish, because in the world there are undoubtedly states that, if all nuclear powers disarmed, would acquire nuclear capabilities so as to hold the world to ransom for their own purposes. If all nuclear weapons were disarmed, nuclear technology, or at least the science behind it, would not just go away.

Such attempts to hold the world to ransom using nuclear weapons would undoubtedly happen if all currently nuclear armed states were to disarm their nuclear weapons, as such attempts are made, to a very limited extent, by some states today. North Korea keeps using its nuclear development programme to attempt to do this, as I point out in Chapter 5. We must remember that the greatest thing that nuclear weapons do today is to deter rogue states from developing their own nuclear weapons, or other weapons of mass destruction with which to try to hold us to ransom.

This thought of the proliferation of nuclear weapons brings us on to the next major point concerning them: nuclear weapons treaties. The nuclear weapons treaty most talked about in the headlines recently has been the Anti-Ballistic Missile Treaty (ABMT). This treaty, signed in 1972, worked on the idea of mutually assured destruction (aptly enough known as MAD). MAD worked on the idea that neither country (in the days when the ABMT was signed the Soviet Union and the USA) would start a nuclear war, as its own cities would be bound by the ABMT to remain unprotected and therefore completely vulnerable to others' nuclear weapons. In other words, so as to ensure that America and the then USSR could obliterate each other without undue hindrance, the ABMT was created to stop the development of a ballistic missile defence system. It seems to me to be completely illogical to keep such a treaty, even now, more than a decade after the fall of the Soviet Union. It is true that there was some point behind the treaty when it was first written, but now the idea that the world is a better place because a strategic ballistic missile defence system cannot be developed is quite ludicrous.

Today the main threat of a nuclear attack, using intercontinental ballistic missiles (ICBM), comes not from another nuclear power, but from a rogue state led by an idealistic, totalitarian dictatorship. The idea of MAD therefore ceases to apply. Such regimes develop (or try to develop) nuclear capabilities not only to hold the world to ransom but also with the intent to use such weapons against us. The reason for their desire to do so varies, but it often stems from (as in North Korea) a hatred of the West (especially of the USA), which is based on some strange idealism, such as Stalinism. But whatever the reasoning behind such a desire, we must be able to defend ourselves against such an attack. The only way to do this is to develop a missile defence system – and that is exactly what the USA has done in the Strategic Defence Initiative (SDI). Such systems are the only way to defend ourselves from an attack by a rogue state using an ICBM (for, most probably, it would be a single ICBM), and thus are the best way that we have of deterring rogue states from developing such weapons of mass destruction in the first place.

Such a system deters rogue states from developing ICBMs and

the weapons to arm them with in the first place, as it greatly lowers the chances of a rogue state's weapons having the desired effect (in other words, striking us) and, by lowering the chances, many rogue states would be deterred from developing ICBMs and weapons of mass destruction (WMD). This idea of other states developing nuclear weapons brings us on to what is probably the most controversial nuclear arms treaty: the Nuclear Non-Proliferation Treaty.

The Nuclear Non-Proliferation Treaty was designed to prevent the proliferation of nuclear weapons. The fact that this treaty was imposed by the United Nations, the five permanent members of which are nuclear-armed states, has opened the treaty up to accusations of hypocrisy. Indeed, such actions do appear ironic and even hypocritical, but the purpose of this treaty is to attempt to stop dangerous, rogue states becoming nuclear-armed. It is true that it is necessary to stop rogue states, such as North Korea, becoming nuclear-armed, but the power of the Nuclear Non-Proliferation Treaty to do so is doubtful. North Korea has shown that if a state wishes to go on trying to obtain nuclear capabilities it can do so, whatever sanctions are imposed to try to stop it. The recent revelation that Iran has been developing the means with which to enrich uranium shows that the Nuclear Non-Proliferation Treaty has very little effect on such rogue states, which are normally the ones trying to develop nuclear weapons anyway. Ultimately, the only thing that will actually stop a rogue state from developing nuclear weapons (or, indeed, other WMDs) is the collapse or overthrow of the regime running that state. Despite being put in place to do a valuable and necessary job, the Nuclear Non-Proliferation Treaty ultimately will not stop a state from developing nuclear weapons.

A world without nuclear weapons is, as Margaret Thatcher put it, 'a fantasy world'.[20] Disarming nuclear weapons would not 'disinvent' nuclear technology. If we and all other nuclear powers were to disarm our nuclear weapons, we would open ourselves up to war-makers in rogue states, which would develop nuclear capabilities so as to hold the world to ransom. It is true that some rogue states may try to develop nuclear technologies anyway, but

---

[20] Thatcher, *Statecraft*.

it is much less likely if we are capable of responding to any nuclear attack by a rogue state in a similar manner. The threat of a full-scale nuclear exchange between nuclear powers may be getting smaller, but the threat of an attack using a nuclear-tipped ICBM from a rogue state is increasing. Therefore, we need to develop a system, such as the American SDI, to defend ourselves from such an attack.

We must accept that the principle of MAD is mad in today's world, and therefore it is time for the ABMT to come to an end. It is also time for us to assess whether the Nuclear Non-Proliferation Treaty is an effective way of stopping rogue states from developing nuclear weapons. The Cold War years of nuclear tension may now be over but nuclear weapons still play a huge role in keeping the peace.

Terrorism

Today, the greatest threat to us and our freedom comes from terrorists and the states that support them. The main aim of most terrorists is, as the name suggests, causing terror so as to advance some political or other goal – be it independence for a region or just to damage the West in general. The atrocities of 11 September 2001 show that some terrorists will stop at nothing to inflict damage on their 'enemies'. We cannot ignore the problem of terrorism and, as such, we must be unflinching in our fight against it. For, if we do not fight it, then not only will the terrorists have effectively won, but they will see it as an open invitation for them to dictate what we can and cannot do through acts of terrorism. Terrorism, in whatever form, cannot be tolerated in free, democratic society, so we must combat it. It must be remembered that, when dealing with terrorism, that it is a crime and therefore terrorists are criminals and should be treated as such. It is very true that, as Margaret Thatcher once said, 'Crime is crime is crime; it is not political.'[21]

But what can be done about terrorism? What we must not do is give in to terrorist demands or simply ignore terrorism. If we give in

---

[21] Quoted on 'Margaret Thatcher', *Wikipedia*, 22 May 2006
<http://en.wikipedia.org/wiki/Margaret_Thatcher>

just once, then the terrorists will continue their activities so as to attempt to dictate to us. If we ignore terrorism, then just as with all other crime, it will not go away and the terrorists will view such a lack of response as a sign of weakness and will continue, or, worse still, step up their activities. What we must do then is to give a strong and continuing response to terrorism. Terrorism is best dealt with by stopping funding reaching it and by stopping regimes that aid terrorism, as I suggest in Chapter 5. Also, we must deal harshly with any terrorist who appears before our courts. We must remember that if any of our citizens fight for a terrorist organisation, then they are giving support to our enemies – effectively, committing treason. The only way that we can truly stop terrorism is by removing those regimes that give it aid and support. We must consider terrorism to be akin to treason and therefore anybody found committing it should be dealt with as such.

Conclusions

- People who stand against the USA, the world's greatest symbol of freedom, stand against capitalism and freedom.

- We in Britain owe our freedom to the USA.

- At least twice in the last century the major threat to our freedom has come from Europe, also at least twice in the last century salvation has come from the USA.

- By supporting the USA we cannot only help to advance our own economy, but we can also help to advance the world economy and therefore freedom.

- The USA is the greatest force for freedom in the world today because of its past and present economic, social, and cultural values.

- In today's world we must remember who our true friends are. God bless America.

- The best way to help the Third World is via trade, not aid.

- By trading with the Third World we help to advance economies and therefore freedoms in those countries.

- For this to work, the rule of law must exist in those countries and their governments must be democratic.

- Capitalism is not the cause of poverty in the Third World – Japan proves this point beyond any reasonable doubt.

- Even though emergency relief is of course necessary, regular handouts to the Third World only cause the Third World to become reliant on such handouts.

- Trading with oppressive regimes will not help the people of those countries – only the overthrow of those regimes will.

- The worst thing that we have exported to the Third World is socialism – not capitalism.

- Nuclear weapons kept the peace during the Cold War and they continue to do so today.

- Those people who call for nuclear disarmament should realise that we cannot 'disinvent' nuclear weapons. A world without nuclear weapons is, quite simply, a 'fantasy world'.

- Nuclear weapons deter hostile nations from carrying out acts of aggression.

- If all the nuclear powers in the world disarmed – as the nuclear-disarmament lobby calls for – then rogue states could easily build their own nuclear weapons with which to hold the world to ransom.

- The Anti-Ballistic Missile Treaty (ABMT) and the principle of mutually assured destruction (MAD) are no longer relevant in today's world.

- Missile defence systems must be developed to deter rogue states, such as North Korea, from attack, and to offer us protection if they do try to attack us.

- The Nuclear Non-Proliferation Treaty can't stop the proliferation of nuclear weapons – the revelations about Iran prove this.

- Our nuclear weapons continue to protect us against aggressive regimes.

- Terrorism is the greatest threat that our freedom faces today.

- We must fight terrorism and we must never give in to terrorism or simply ignore it. Such actions can only lead to further atrocities.

- The best way to deal with terrorism is to remove the regimes that support it.

- When dealing with terrorists who fight against our state we must remember that we are dealing with criminals who have committed a crime that is akin to treason.

Chapter 5
ROGUE STATES

Introduction

The best way to stop terrorism is to stop it from gaining funding and support, and the only way to stop terrorism from gaining funding and support is to destroy the regimes that give terrorism funding and support. Regimes that support terrorism are normally deeply set against capitalism and free society and are willing to develop technologies (i.e. nuclear) with which to damage the West. Such states are the true rogue states, but as well as the threat that these states pose to us, we must remember that these are very often oppressive dictatorships that rule by fear and whose people do not know – and, very often, have not known – freedom. By ending such regimes, not only do we end the threat to ourselves, but we also free an entire nation. By allowing them to trade freely and have a democratic government, we allow the people of that nation the opportunity to build their own future, where they can do what they want (that is of course, within the rule of law), and by means of free industry and trade, to progress into a brighter future.

In this chapter I aim to highlight the worst rogue states in the world, and to show what a danger they are to us, how these states are run, and why, ultimately, these regimes must collapse or be overthrown.

The Iraqi Victory

As I have said earlier, freedom is the most important right, and therefore must be preserved at all costs. So, bringing about the end of a regime that denied its people their right to freedom, as happened in Iraq, is in itself perfectly justified. By bringing about the end of Saddam Hussein and his evil regime, coalition forces gave freedom to an entire nation. Despite the fact that the people of Iraq no longer have to live in fear of this madman, people say that we should never have gone to war with Iraq because no weapons of mass destruction (WMDs) were found (and, according to the Butler report, are unlikely ever to be found). But surely the liberation of millions of people from oppression in addition to the fact that Saddam had used and still threatened to use chemical weapons, was sufficient justification for war. Of course, that is not to say that if the government did knowingly deceive Parliament and the nation over Iraqi WMDs, then no actions should be taken. However, those who say that the Iraq war was wrong might like to be reminded of Saddam's history and how he ran his country.

It was always clear that Saddam was a ruthless tyrant who needed to be removed from power, but it was only after Iraq was finally liberated that the true horrors of Saddam's regime came to light. It was already well known that Saddam killed at least one million of his own Kurdish population by turning his chemical weapons on them in the Iran–Iraq War. The fact that Saddam was willing to use chemical weapons in this way not only shows what an evil tyrant he was, but it also shows that Saddam was willing to use WMDs, which, as I will show later, meant that Saddam's chemical weapons were a real threat.

When Iraq was liberated from Saddam's regime, every town into which the coalition forces went showed evidence of Saddam's tyrannous regime. Towns were considered incomplete unless they had their very own statue of Saddam gracing the main square. People were banned from watching satellite television, lest they gain ideas that were not Ba'ath party policy. Such signs of oppression were there for all to see on Iraq's streets, but as coalition forces looked deeper into what was left of Saddam's Iraq, they found evidence of the heinous crimes that had been committed under his regime. As well as a statue of Saddam to remind everybody who was in charge, every town appears to have had its own torture chamber for those who dared to think, let alone step out of line. After the liberation of Iraq, pictures of people crowding outside police stations and jails to see if there was any trace of their loved ones became all too familiar sights. Sadly, often the only trace that remained was a seized identity card. Then, if that were not enough evidence of the crimes that Saddam and his regime had perpetrated, mass graves were found near Basra. And people still say that it was wrong to go to war with Iraq.

Saddam's appalling human rights record was reason enough to remove him from power, but, in addition, his record with WMDs and his willingness to use them was so lamentable that it would have been folly to leave him in charge. In the eight-year Iran–Iraq War, Saddam showed no hesitation in using chemical weapons against his own people, let alone foreigners, so the thought that Saddam would have not dared use them against the West is complete idiocy. In the first Gulf War, Saddam launched Scud missiles against Israel, which came very close to launching its own, nuclear response. The fact that Saddam was willing to attack a nuclear power shows what a dangerous madman he was and that he would have been more than willing to attack us if he had had the capabilities. To think that a person who used chemical weapons against his own people and launched a conventional attack on a nuclear-armed ally of America did not pose a risk to us is insane. Any person with such a history, who kept up a relentless barrage of anti-Western propaganda, would, quite clearly, if they had the means at their disposal, launch an attack against the West or its interests abroad.

Saddam's history with WMDs was more than enough to show that he was a danger to us and needed to be stopped. However, it must be understood that whilst Saddam's human rights record and his past with chemical weapons was reason enough to remove him from power, if the government lied in or 'sexed up' the Iraq weapons dossier (which, despite Mr Blair's exoneration in the Hutton Enquiry, has been left a possibility by the Butler Report), such deception is completely unacceptable in a modern democracy. Rather than using very shaky evidence or even 'finding' evidence of Saddam's WMDs, the Blair government should have realised that Saddam's past record was enough evidence to go to war with him and most certainly did not need sexing up. Indeed, instead of using such uncertain evidence of Saddam's WMDs, the government should have turned to Saddam's past for evidence against him. Saddam's aggression against Kuwait in 1990 was not part of a religious jihad, as Saddam claimed, but was part of a calculated attempt on Saddam's part to hold the world to ransom. If Saddam's aggression had not been checked and he had been allowed to advance all the way down the Persian Gulf, he would have controlled around 60 per cent of the world's oil and thus would have been able to hold us to ransom. This was yet another part of Saddam's insane drive for more power.

Thankfully the days of Saddam Hussein are over and the Gulf no longer need fear being overrun by this madman. As Saddam is no longer there to try to take over the world oil resources, the Middle East, and therefore the world as a whole is more stable. Despite some people's claims that the Iraq War was a terrible disaster, it was really a victory for freedom. With Saddam gone we now have one less dangerous rogue state to cope with and we now know for certain that Saddam cannot harm us with the WMDs that he so loved to talk about. But, the greatest victory that has been won in Iraq is that a whole nation has been freed from a corrupt, oppressive regime that denied them virtually all freedoms. And, as well as achieving the victory of allowing a whole people the chance to build a better future for themselves, we have won another victory – a victory that is already being felt well outside Iraq's borders. By defeating an evil, oppressive dictator who delighted in threatening others and bringing him to face justice – justice that he denied to so many of his own people – we have sent a powerful message to all other such states in the world.

Libya

It is clear that this warning from Iraq has already reached the leaders of some rogue states. Colonel Muammar Gaddafi, who for many years was deeply hostile to the West, has suddenly decided to be more open and has admitted Libya's guilt for a terrorist act committed against us. It is no coincidence that this U-turn in stances coincided with Saddam Hussein's capture. The pictures of Saddam shortly after he had been dragged from his hole clearly sent a potent warning to Gaddafi – either stop being hostile to the

West, or end up being dragged out of a hole by American troops as Saddam was. Despite this sudden admission of guilt for acts of terrorism committed by Libya, the country still sends out conflicting messages, for, as Gaddafi opens up and admits Libya's responsibility for the bombing of Pan Am flight 103 over Lockerbie, his prime minister, Shukri Ghanem, says that Libya only made these concessions so as to buy peace. These conflicting messages coming from Libya should start alarm bells ringing, since this is similar to Saddam Hussein's actions in Iraq. And, as with Saddam, Gaddafi's past record provides an illuminating insight into how he runs his country and what his likely action will be.

Colonel Gaddafi runs his country – the Great Arab People's Libyan Jamahiriya – according to the ideas contained within his book, *The Green Book* (rather like Mao's *Little Red Book*). The three volumes of this book explain how Gaddafi thinks that the world, not only Libya, should be run. In this book, he not only denounces capitalism but also communism and goes on to say that the world should be run according to the 'Third International Way'. One cannot help wondering what similarities there are between Gaddafi's third way and Blair's third way. Gaddafi's third way is rather foggy in its definition – so there are similarities between the two third ways! Gaddafi recently summed up what he thought the Third International Way is. In an interview he said:

> It was simply an attempt to explain the dialectic which exists be-
> tween Marxism and capitalism. The world has reached a political
> and economic impasse, and humanity simply cannot accept this
> impasse and accept to die. There must be a way out. That way out
> is this new theory.[22]

The fact that Gaddafi frequently comes out with such statements begs the question 'Is Gaddafi mad?' The answer is probably yes, but does it really matter? Gaddafi is in charge of Libya, mad or not.

---

[22] 'Heart to Heart With Qadhafi', *New Africa*, February 1983, quoted in 'Muammar Al Qadhafi: The Consummate Revolutionary Leader of the World Revolution', Revolutionary Committee Movement, Australia, 2006.
<http://www.mathaba.net/info/mqadhafi.htm>

Gaddafi's strange political philosophy, his sudden U-turn and his apparent madness, should make us very wary in our dealings with him. On top of this, we must remember that Gaddafi's human rights record most certainly leaves something to be desired. As recently as 1996, his regime was responsible for mass killings in Abu Salim prison, where many prisoners – including political prisoners – were killed in a single day. Despite the fact that some progress has been made with the release of some political prisoners, many people are said just to 'die' in prison. Naturally, the cause of death is never made public. Add to this the numerous 'disappearances' that take place in Libya, the fact that nobody whatsoever can vote, and that no political parties are allowed, that all the Libyan press is state controlled and that nobody is allowed to criticise state policy, it is clear that Libya is far from being free or democratic.

This lack of democracy should instantly make us wary in our dealings with Libya, but what should make us most wary in our dealings with Gaddafi is his past attempts to develop weapons of mass destruction, intended for use against the West, and Libya's past support of terrorist acts. Libya, by its own admission, has tried to acquire the capabilities to enrich uranium and has previously built up a stockpile of chemical and probably biological weapons. Despite the positive step of Libya sending its nuclear weapons development material to us, we must remember that even with regular inspections, a chemical weapons programme is not difficult to conceal in a country the size of Libya. Complete openness on Libya's part to weapons inspectors is a great step in the right direction, but given Gaddafi's past we must not disregard Libya as a threat.

What has caused Libya to be so isolated from the rest of the world is not sanctions because of its WMD programmes, but its past support of terrorism. Recently Prime Minister Shukri Ghanem accepted responsibility for the bombing of Pan Am flight 103 over Lockerbie, and agreed to pay compensation to the victims' families. However the sincerity of this admission is thrown into doubt after his comments made in a *Today* programme interview:

> We thought that it was easier to buy peace and this is why we agreed to compensation ... I say we bought peace.[23]

Despite this comment being retracted by Libyan authorities, the fact that a senior Libyan official could, in public, take such an attitude, shows that Libya's new-found warmth to the West might not be entirely sincere. A regime that has at any point orchestrated acts of terrorism against any one country must be regarded with deep suspicion. If it later admits responsibility for that act, but then makes a statement contrary to that expression of guilt (even if that statement is later retracted), then that state should be regarded with even more suspicion. This buying of peace with the West, as Dr Ghanem put it, may show that Libya has finally realised that they need the outside world far more than the outside world needs Libya. If Libya is sincere in its recent actions, then all is well and good, but if not then we must only proceed with the utmost caution.

This acceptance from Libya that it needs the outside world has come about because of the war with Iraq. When Saddam's regime was overthrown it would have become obvious to Gaddafi that either he must cooperate or face a similar fate to Saddam. Gaddafi's new-found warmth to us, which the Iraq War undoubtedly brought about, is definitely a step in the right direction for Libya. However, Libya's past, its lack of democracy and Dr Ghanem's comments should make us very wary when dealing with Libya. For Libya to leave the rogue state category and to fully cease to be considered our enemy, it must not only stop its WMD programmes and its support of terrorism, but it also must open itself up to democracy, which is the only way a government can truly be held to account. I fear that such democracy will never be possible in a Libya under Colonel Gaddafi's rule.

North Korea

There are rogue states and then there is North Korea. The People's Democratic [sic] Republic of Korea is probably the most

---

[23] Quoted on 'Shukri Ghanem', *Wikipedia*, 05 June 2006.
<http://en.wikipedia.org/wiki/Shukri_Ghanem>

dangerous of all the rogue states in the world for the simple reason that it is run by a hardline communist doctrine dictatorship. This regime, which is currently headed by Kim Jong-il, who is the son of Kim Il-sung, the North Korean leader in the Korean War of the early 1950s, seeks continuously to develop WMDs and ultimately strives to use them against the West or the West's allies. The regime of Pyongyang was founded by Kim Il-sung, who, despite being dead, still holds official office in North Korea as the 'eternal president'. Kim Il-sung came to power two years before the Korean War, which claimed an estimated 1.3 million lives. The Korean War divided the Korean peninsula into its current form, with the free and democratic South and the communist and oppressed North. To this day along the divide between the two Koreas, North and South Korean troops face each other in case of a restart of hostilities, which were never brought to an official end. On the northern side of the border we know very little of what life is like, but given the fact that the incumbent regime is socialist and totalitarian, and from the little bit of information that has leaked out of the North, we can have some idea of the suffering that goes on in the People's Democratic Republic of Korea.

One of the few things that is clear about North Korea is that the regime of Pyongyang rules by a combination of fear and brainwashing – just like virtually all other communist states. The only official pictures to come out of North Korea are those that show happy, cheering crowds at official ceremonies, or those showing what most money is spent on in North Korea – the army. Any North Korean allowed to speak to Western journalists would say that the terrible famine that the North is currently suffering is due to 'American imperialism', not Pyongyang's bizarre ideology of socialist self-sufficiency (known as 'Juche'). Such reports and images (that is, official North Korean reports and pictures) and the fact that 1.6 million people have died in party purges and in the North Korean concentration camps since the communists took over in 1948, show that the government of the People's Democratic Republic of Korea rules in a way that is as far as possible from the manner that is suggested by the country's name.

This mass murder and blatant oppression that goes on in North Korea because of its paranoid communist government would be bad enough, but North Korea has recently been hit by the above-mentioned famine, which has claimed countless lives. This disaster has been exacerbated by Pyongyang's strange socialist policies. As Kim Jong-il well knows, all of his power rests with his army, so, even though his people are starving, he will make sure that the army receives more food than the civilian population of his country. Thus, Kim Jong-il is even willing to bend the rules of 'Juche', as it were, so as to receive international food aid, but any such aid that he receives goes straight to his army, not his civilian population. Thirty per cent of North Korea's GDP is spent on the army, which shows that Kim cares far more about his hold on power than 'the people'. As in all communist countries, the question of 'who are the people?' appears in North Korea.

Kim Jong-il's military craze goes far beyond the realm of the dictator trying to remain in power and enters the realm of the regime trying to blackmail the international community into doing its bidding. Why Pyongyang should do this, is quite honestly, a mystery. It is not as though Pyongyang would spend any money it received from doing so to improve conditions for its people – its past record shows that any extra wealth that North Korea receives would go straight to the military. The most probable explanation is that Kim Jong-il is mad. He may have some insane plan to return the world to the 'glory days' of communism, but, as in the case of Colonel Gaddafi, it does not really matter. Kim Jong-il is still in charge of North Korea.

What we must do, therefore, is to look at the threat posed to us by North Korea and then work out what we must and must not do. As well as having a massive army, North Korea is pushing to develop ICBM capabilities to reach America and her allies. Alongside this ICBM programme, which has already produced the Taepodong long-range missile that is capable of reaching North Korea's most likely victim, Japan, North Korea has also developed and frequently exports to countries such as Syria, Egypt and Vietnam, a surface to surface Scud-type missile. North Korea has, on top of this, produced the Nodong intermediate-range missile which is a definite threat to her other likely victim, South Korea. But alone all these missiles are useless, whatever their range. Therefore North Korea's other main development line is WMDs with which to arm its missiles. The WMDs that Pyongyang would most like to get its hands on are nuclear weapons.

Unlike other rogue states that have tried to develop WMDs, North Korea would be likely – or, more accurately, mad enough – to actually use them against us. Those who dismiss such statements as hyperbole may like to consider the fact that every day, the civilian population of Pyongyang descends into deep, subterranean bunkers in order to practise for a nuclear attack on Pyongyang. A regime not planning to use WMD, moreover nuclear weapons, would not go through such action, however mad that regime was. In addition to this evidence, which is, to say the least, damning, Pyongyang has periodically claimed, then later denied, having a nuclear weapons programme and even nuclear weapons. Sites for the development of nuclear weapons have been seen within North Korea, so with all this evidence we can safely assume that Pyongyang is trying to develop nuclear weapons (or other WMDs) with which to attempt to blackmail us and ultimately to use against us. Personally, at this moment in time, I do not believe that North Korea has any nuclear weapons. If they had, they would have used them.

Most rogue states use WMDs they actually have (or claim to have) to attempt to blackmail the West, as was the case with Saddam Hussein in Iraq. However, North Korea is, yet again, the exception. As Pyongyang is clearly insane enough to actually use any WMDs that it manages to acquire against us, it would use its WMD development schemes to try to blackmail us. As such, North Korean official media recently announced that North Korea would 'continue developing, testing and deploying missiles' although America and the West could stop this if they were to 'make compensation for losses.'[24]

Pyongyang later set this compensation to start at around $1 billion per year. Such a reckless statement not only proves that North Korea has a WMD programme, but that it would also be

---

[24] Nicholas Eberstadt, 'The Most Dangerous Country', *National Interest*, Autumn 1999, quoted in Thatcher, *Statecraft*.

willing to use any of the WMDs that it produced. It also shows what a terrible threat North Korea is to us; that Pyongyang would be more than happy to use WMDs on us and, above all it shows just how crazy Kim Jong-il and his regime are.

As the above statement testifies, North Korea is a real threat to us and therefore shows us that we must be tough in our stance towards it. North Korea's past record of making deals so as to get aid that is later used on the military should make us very wary of any apparent concessions Pyongyang appears to make.

If any further reason why we should be cautious about any apparent concessions from Pyongyang is required, then one only has to look at the case of the light-water nuclear reactors. In 1994, North Korea and the USA came to an agreement where Pyongyang would freeze its nuclear programme in return for an annual half million tonnes of free oil and two light-water nuclear reactors. Despite this agreement, Pyongyang did not even slow down its nuclear programme. Such blatant hypocrisy should make us very wary indeed of Pyongyang's apparent 'peace deals'.

It is clear that we must not take Pyongyang at its word and that we must not give in to them, as happened when the USA gave them two light-water reactors in 1994. As for what we should do to make North Korea safer and to make it better for its population, the best, most favourable option is just to wait. The fact that North Korea no longer has the USSR for support and that its economy is already in ruins means that the regime in Pyongyang will collapse, perhaps (hopefully) in similar circumstances to those in which the Berlin Wall fell. When Kim Jong-il's regime falls (by whatever means) we will know the full horrors that have been perpetrated in North Korea. Given Korea's violent past however, it sadly seems unlikely that the transition between oppression and freedom for North Korea's people will be bloodless. North Korea's bizarre Stalinist regime is a real threat to us and until it falls we cannot ignore it. Hopefully the fall of communism in North Korea will be peaceful. However if North Korea attacks us, our interests or allies (or, for that matter, appears to be about to do so) we must not be afraid of responding to that attack and bringing down Kim Jong-il and his regime by whatever means necessary.

Iran

Iran, like North Korea, is another state that it is instinctively anti-Western and ruled by what is essentially a doctrine dictatorship. However, unlike North Korea, Iran's doctrine dictatorship is theocratic. Iran's rulers run Iran according to an extreme Islamic revolutionary doctrine that leaves very little room for democracy, or freedom of speech or thought. Again, like so many other states that pose a threat to us, Iran is run by an oppressive, undemocratic government. It is indeed true to say that such states can only really cease to be a threat to us when they are democratically governed, as only with democracy can a government that serves the people of a country, not some anti-Western doctrine, be elected. Of course, that is not to say that democratic states cannot be a threat to us (although I find it hard to name one democratic state that is hostile to us) and also not to say that undemocratic countries cannot be pro-Western (as Iran was under the Shah).

The trouble with Iran really began in 1979 with the overthrow of the pro-Western Shah who, for several years, had been following a series of modernising, westernising reforms on Iran (Persia). The Shah was replaced by the Islamic revolutionary leader Ayatollah Khomeini who had been exiled to Paris. With the Ayatollah's return, an Islamic Republic was declared and with that Iran began to be governed by an extremely oppressive theocracy. Shortly after this, Iran's history becomes intertwined with that of Iraq, as Saddam Hussein launched an attack on Iran in 1979 that led to the eight-year Iran–Iraq War. As the regime of the Ayatollah Khomeini progressed, the abuses of people's freedoms began as they invariably do in such a dictatorship.

The regime in Tehran is responsible for various crimes against humanity. These mainly concern people who have dared to speak out against the oppressive regime, being unfairly 'tried' in secret before being executed, imprisoned or in some other way tortured. Indeed, even such a mockery of a trial is not necessary to sanction torture or indefinite imprisonment in Iran. Iran is well known for using lashing and amputation as a punishment; that quite clearly shows what sort of regime it is operating.

The case of Amir Abbas Fakhravar shows that the regime is ruthless and willing to go to any lengths to achieve its ends. Amir Abbas Fakhravar was not only beaten before a court and then denied medical treatment; he was also subjected to what can only be described as physiological torture. The following is the Amnesty International report on his treatment at the 125 detention centre in Tehran.

> His cell in the 125 detention centre reportedly had no windows, and was entirely coloured creamy white, as were his clothes. At meal times, he was reportedly given white rice on white, disposable paper plates and if he needed to use the toilet, he had to put a white slip of paper under the door of the cell to alert guards, who reportedly had footwear designed to muffle any sound. He was forbidden to speak to anyone.
>
> Amnesty International has been told that the 'silence is deafening' in the facility and that this technique of sensory deprivation is called 'white torture' (*shekanjeh-e sefid*).[25]

A regime that is brutal enough to subject its people to this, and other types of barbaric torture and that denies the right to freedom of speech and the right to a fair trial is clearly a threat to us. These acts show the ruthlessness of the regime in Tehran and also show that it will stop at nothing. The way in which the regime runs Iran and its willingness to use torture against its own people shows that it has very little respect for human life, which we in the West hold so dear. A regime that is so brutal to its own people is a threat to us because its brutal, stop-at-nothing attitude, applies to its foreign as well as domestic policies. Tehran has said that it is reforming its penal system to stop such abuses taking place, but until results are actually visible we must be sceptical of such statements as they may well only be there to buy favour. The way in which the regime abuses human rights should make us very wary in our dealings with Iran for as it is willing to attack its own people's basic human rights, then it may be willing to attack us with the

---

[25] 'Iran: Amir Abbas Fakhravar, freelance journalist and prisoner of conscience', *Amnesty International UK*, 13 February 2004.
<http://www.amnesty.org.uk/news/press/15199.shtml>

weapons of mass destruction that it has sought so desperately to obtain.

Iran has, for a long time, tried to obtain nuclear weapons and the capabilities to produce them. Despite being a signatory to the 1970 Nuclear Non-Proliferation Treaty, Iran continues to try to produce nuclear weapons by producing ever-changing excuses to try to keep the International Atomic Energy Agency (IAEA) inspectors at bay. Tehran claims that its forays into the world of nuclear energy are 'peaceful and transparent'. However, given that Iran does not even have enough uranium to run one nuclear reactor for its lifetime and that Tehran recently unveiled its centrifuge to enrich uranium sufficiently to make it suitable for nuclear weapons, the peacefulness of its nuclear programme seems to vanish into thin air. Iran's nuclear weapons research is definitely going on and most certainly, if it were ultimately successful, is a threat to the region and the world as a whole. Not only this, but the fact that Tehran is getting away with the research is damaging to the credibility of the IAEA and the Nuclear Non-Proliferation Treaty as far as stopping the world-wide proliferation of nuclear weapons is concerned.

It is not even as though Iran's nuclear weapons research is done with the utmost secrecy or in a way that could be mistaken for research into 'peaceful' nuclear technologies. For example, it has recently come to light that Iran has an advanced gas-powered P2 centrifuge, a device used to make highly enriched weapons-grade uranium. Tehran initially claimed that the centrifuge had only been used with non-nuclear materials. However, an IAEA inspection of this, the Natanz centrifuge facility, found traces of highly enriched uranium present at the site. At this point, Tehran changed from saying that this centrifuge programme had been running since 1997, to saying that it had been running since 1987 and since it had acquired parts from foreign sources, the highly enriched uranium must have come from those foreign parts. Even the most incompetent government does not 'lose' ten years and does not fail to mention in reports to the IAEA that parts of a P2 centrifuge came from foreign sources unless, of course, they are changing their story to try to cover up the truth. Tehran last year halted its nuclear weapons programme, but it has indicated that this move is only temporary.

It is clear that Iran is attempting to develop nuclear capabilities and given the nature of the regime, it is clear that any such weapons would be a threat to us. As George W Bush made clear, a nuclear armed Iran cannot be allowed to happen.[26] If Iran keeps up its disregard for its treaty commitments and continues in the way it has been doing with regard to nuclear research, its case must be referred to the UN Security Council for immediate action.

However, Iran's nuclear weapons policy is not the only threat that Iran poses. Despite being party to a treaty outlawing it, Iran has chemical weapons capabilities. According to the testimony of US Assistant Secretary for Verification and Compliance, Paula De Stutter, made before the US–Israeli Joint Parliament Committee on 17 September 2003, Iran is believed to have had manufactured 'a wide variety of chemical agents and weaponised some of these agents in artillery shells, mortars, rockets and aerial bombs'.[27] Though this manufacture took place before Iran joined the Chemical Weapons Convention, it has still kept its chemical weapons stockpiles, an act that is prohibited by the treaty. In fact not only does Iran have a stockpile of chemical weapons it may also be attempting to modernise them. A recent non-compliance report by the US government concluded:

> Iran has not submitted a complete and accurate declaration and, in fact, is acting to modernise key elements of its chemical weapons programme...[28]

As Iran has clearly failed to comply with the Chemical Weapons Convention and as reports into Iran have concluded that Iran has and is trying to update these weapons, it is clear that it has and, in the case of nuclear weapons, is trying to obtain,

---

[26] 'Iranian WMD and Support of Terrorism, Testimony of Paula De Stutter, US Assistant Secretary for Verification and Compliance', Before the US–Israeli Joint Parliamentary Committee, Washington, DC, 17 September 2003, *US Department of State*, <http://www.state.gov/t/vci/rls/rm/24494.htm>.

[27] Ibid.

[28] US Government Noncomplicance Report, quoted in Ibid.

capabilities that are a threat to us. However, as if failing to comply with the Nuclear Non-Proliferation Treaty, the IAEA and the Chemical Weapons Convention was not enough, Iran has had to breach just one more international weapons limitation treaty. Another US non-compliance report has determined that Iran has produced biological weapons, which is in breach of its commitments to the Biological Weapons Convention. Iran, the non-compliance report has determined, has some biological agents and the means to deploy them. Again, Iran has tried to cover its tracks by attempting to conceal its biological weapons within its extensive biotech and pharmaceutical industries. The breach of yet another convention shows just how desperate Iran is to obtain WMDs, but, of course, WMDs are useless without a means of delivery.

Iran has therefore, with help from entities within Russia, China and, of course, North Korea, developed a variety of ballistic missiles with which to launch its weapons of mass destruction. The missile with the longest range (1,300 km), the Shahab-3, could quite easily reach Israel, American forces within Iraq and Afghanistan and British troops stationed on Cyprus. The fact that Tehran is pushing forward with the development of its ICBMs and intermediate-range ballistic missiles (IRBM) shows quite clearly that Iran is trying to enlarge its 'sphere of influence' by using WMDs. If the development of such ballistic missile technologies is kept up by Iran, it may soon be able to hit targets within Western Europe and even the USA. As Tehran is pushing to obtain ballistic missiles with ever increasing ranges, it is clear that it is not developing these weapons with defence against hostile neighbours in mind. The fact that Iran is striving to obtain nuclear weapons capabilities alongside this long-range missile development programme makes it clear that Iran wants to be able to threaten us, or even use WMDs against us. The possibility of an actual Iranian attack on us is made even more likely when one takes into account the terrorist factor.

The regime in Tehran has most definitely been involved in terrorist activities; the US state department describes Iran as being 'the most active state sponsor of terrorism'.[29] Indeed the recent 9/11 commission report concluded that Iran may have even played its part in the 11 September attacks. The Iranian Islamic Revolutionary Guard Corps and the Ministry of Security and Intelligence (the Iranian governmental authority responsible for most of the human rights abuses that take place within Iran) is believed to have been actively involved in the planning of terrorist acts. Tehran is also known to have provided a safe haven, training, and weapons to terrorist groups including Lebanese Hizballah, HAMAS, the Palestinian Islamic Jihad, and the Popular Liberation Front for Palestine General Command. On top of this, the Ayatollah's regime is also believed to provide aid and comfort to Ansar al-Islam terrorists and, it is thought, senior al-Qaeda figures. Add to this the fact that Tehran is strongly opposed to the Middle East peace process – indeed it has described Israel as a 'cancerous tumour' and frequently describes America as 'the great Satan' – it is easy to conclude that Tehran takes the same view as many of the terrorist groups that it supports: that America and Western civilisation should be destroyed. This coupled with the Ayatollah's regime's lack of respect for human rights and, indeed, human life in general, makes Iran one of the most worrying rogue states in the world.

The regime in Tehran is no doubt responsible for appalling human rights abuses, although we may not find out their full extent while the Ayatollah's regime is in place. The fact that Tehran's statements on its weapons of mass destruction vary so widely shows that Tehran must be striving to further develop its WMDs. Coupled with this, Iran's drive to create ballistic missiles capable of reaching our shores and beyond surely means that Tehran is developing its WMDs, and moreover its nuclear capabilities that it strives to use offensively rather than defensively. Add to this Tehran's support for terrorist groups that work against us, it is clear that Iran is a real threat to global security. Former president Hojjatoleslam Val Moslemin Sayed Mohammad Khatami may have called for an end to human rights abuses in Iran, but we must wait and see if Iran really does reform

---

[29] Ibid.

on this particular ground, which is yet another point that makes it threatening to global security.

We must be very sceptical of any 'offers' with regards to its WMD programmes, which, as past experience of Iran tells us, they will do almost anything to keep. The case of the P2 centrifuge and the missing ten years should be proof of this. Any concession that Iran appears to make may just be another stalling tactic brought about by the fear that the regime shares with the regime in Tripoli – ending up the same way as Saddam Hussein. We must only believe that Tehran is genuine in any claims it makes when and only when it starts to openly destroy its nuclear weapons, when it allows IAEA and UN inspectors free access to confirm this and when it gives the whole truth about its WMD programmes and existing WMDs – something that will again have to be confirmed by IAEA and UN inspectors. Only then and provided that Tehran begins to follow the road to democratic reforms and freedom which it has pledged support for, can we allow Iran to cease to be considered an enemy.

However, as in Libya, I fear that this may never happen under the incumbent regime. We must therefore look at other options. By imposing sanctions on Iran we may eventually force it to see sense – as appears to be the case in Libya. But this stage may take many years to arrive at and indeed may never arrive at all. Sanctions against Iran are undoubtedly the best option as, without international trade and aid, Iran's economy, infrastructure and most probably the Ayatollah's regime would collapse, which would bring about an end to the Iranian threat. However, given Iran's desire to obtain nuclear weapons and given that sanctions have not stopped other countries (i.e. North Korea) from developing nuclear programmes, we must be aware of the possibility that Iran may become nuclear-armed before sanctions alone can stop it becoming so. Of course a nuclear-armed Iran must never be allowed to happen as, given the Iranian regime's support for terrorism – especially its part in the 11 September attacks – it would have a terrible destabilising effect on the whole world, let alone the Middle East. So, even though stopping Iran's development of WMDs and support of terrorism, through sanctions, may be the most desirable option, if it ever comes to light that Iran definitely was involved in the 11 September attacks or that it is on the verge of becoming nuclear armed, we must not hesitate in disarming Iran by force.

In Our Interests

The rogue states mentioned in this chapter are just a few of the states that sponsor terrorism and are set instinctively against us. As well as their hatred of the West and Western values and their desire to obtain weapons of mass destruction, all these states share another common feature – they are all dictatorial states that oppress their people. Indeed, one of the main arguments for why we should impose sanctions, or even remove a regime altogether, is because it is oppressive and has little regard for human rights. Some people may ask why we should take such action, when, although it oppresses its own people, a regime does not pose a direct threat to our interests or us. Personally, I should hope that it is clear to all why we should not condone or simply ignore such states. Such states are likely to pose a risk to us anyway, as they value freedom so little that they would surely not hold our basic values very highly. They would therefore be set against our values and against us. Because of their oppressive nature, such states normally have no economic freedom either, which means that their economies are most likely in ruins. Therefore these states require aid, which costs us money.

The monetary costs of such oppressive states brings us on to the economic reasons why we should stand against them. As I said earlier, these states normally have no economic freedom and therefore their economies are often in ruins, so humanitarian aid is necessary to prevent even more death and suffering in that country. However, if these oppressive regimes were replaced with democratic regimes that allowed economic freedom so the economies became more sound, then aid would not be required. This would not only save us money, but would also stop the poverty cycle in those countries which is perpetuated by a reliance on Western handouts, as described in Chapter 4.

The other reason why we should aim to convert oppressive, undemocratic states into free and democratic is that the people of that country will become freer as their economy progresses, as I explained in Chapter 1. Indeed, this is the most important reason why we must stand against oppression in favour of freedom and democracy for, as we give freedom – both individual and economic – to a nation, we allow a whole people to enjoy this most important right of all.

The regimes of most rogue states are politically unstable and/or economically unviable and will probably, given time, collapse of their own accord. However, during this time – which may be a long time – rogue states still have the potential to cause serious damage to us either by supporting terrorism or by developing and using some form of WMD. We can limit a country's capacity to do these things by imposing sanctions such as trade embargoes, and by limiting aid supplies to an absolute minimum in order to prevent a humanitarian crisis. Such emergency aid should be in the form of supplies only and its distribution should be carefully monitored. What has happened in North Korea should be reason enough for this.

But even with such measures in place to stop rogue states developing WMDs and supporting terrorism, such a state may still carry out an attack against us – be it through terrorism or another means – or it may become apparent that the state has the capabilities to attack us and is willing to use them. In addition to this it may become apparent that a state is providing a safe haven for terrorists (or has done so in the past) and is supporting terrorist actions against us, even if the state is not directly behind any act of terrorism (e.g. Iran). In all of the above circumstances, the only option that we really would have left open to us is to disarm and remove the regime of that state by force. Such action may sound drastic in the extreme, but if an attack were carried out against us and we were not responsive, a rogue state might regard it as an invitation to dictate what we could and could not do. As with terrorism,[30] we must be robust in our response to any such attack. Equally, we must not be afraid of using pre-emptive strikes to disarm and remove regimes that have or are likely to have the capabilities with which to cause us harm. When all is said and done, we must not be afraid to use force against any state that

---

[30] See p.51.

attacks us, or is likely to attack us (or is likely to develop and use capabilities with which to attack us), whether an attack be through direct or indirect support of terrorism or any other means whatsoever. In other words, we must never fail to defend ourselves against attack and we must never allow dangerous states to develop dangerous capabilities.

Conclusions

- Terrorism can only be stopped by stopping its sources of funding and support.

- The rogue states that aid and support terrorism are those with a deep ideological hatred of the West.

- Very often such rogue states seek to develop WMDs and the means to deploy them against us.

- Such states are often run by oppressive doctrine dictatorships that are not at all representative of their people (as in Iraq).

- If the West has to remove a rogue regime from power, not only does it protect itself from a threat to freedom, but it also gives a people the chance to enjoy the most important right of all.

- Removing Saddam Hussein from power was a victory; not only did it give the Iraqi people freedom and protect the world from a dangerous madman, but it also served as a warning to the leaders of rogue states throughout the world – this is nowhere more apparent than in Libya.

- Of course, that is not to say that if the government did deceive Parliament and the public about Iraqi WMDs, such an act should not go unpunished.

- Colonel Gaddafi's regime in Libya did, for a long time, sponsor terrorism and attempt to acquire the capabilities with which to attack us.

- Gaddafi's regime is responsible for torture and other acts of oppression.

- Gaddafi's recent positive steps are to be welcomed, but comments such as Dr Ghanem's should make us wary.

- If Libya is truly willing to reform then all is well and good, but past experiences with Libya should make us very cautious.

- Libya can only be considered to be completely safe when it is free and democratic – something that I doubt is possible under Colonel Gaddafi.

- By far the most dangerous of all the rogue states is North Korea.

- Like many other rogue regimes, North Korea is trying to develop WMDs (especially nuclear weapons). The difference is that North Korea's leader might actually be mad enough to use them.

- North Korea's communist regime has a deep hatred of America and Western capitalism and what we would consider to be freedom in general. That is why it is the most dangerous of all the rogue states.

- Pyongyang is quite happy to lie about its capabilities so as to obtain aid for its army.

- Any apparent concessions made by Pyongyang are just attempts to buy time with which to develop its WMDs and ballistic missiles with which it would attempt to blackmail us (indeed it has already tried) or worse still that it would actually use against us or our interests.

- We must not be held to ransom by Pyongyang and we must defend ourselves and our allies against Pyongyang's madness by whatever means necessary.

- North Korea will only cease to be a threat when the regime in Pyongyang falls, which, as it is communist, is bound to happen. This may happen in a 'Berlin Wall' style, but given the North's incumbent regime and Korea's recent past, it is more likely to be a very bloody affair.

- Iran is another state with an extreme doctrine dictatorship that is deeply hostile to the West.

- The regime is responsible for terrible human rights abuses in Iran – those who dare to speak out often 'disappear' without trace.

- The way that the regime abuses the rights and freedoms of its own people should immediately make us realise that it will stop at nothing.

- Iran's nuclear research is not 'peaceful and transparent' as Tehran claims, but is another move to develop WMDs and is a clear violation of the Nuclear Non-Proliferation Treaty.

- Iran's reports to the IAEA clearly do not contain the whole truth. The case of the P2 centrifuge and the 'missing' ten years is proof of this.

- Iran has modernised and continues to modernise its chemical weapons stockpile, which is a flagrant breach of the Chemical Weapons Convention.

- Iran has breached the Biological Weapons Convention by producing biological weapons.

- Iran tries to do this under cover of its biotech industry. One cannot help but be reminded of Saddam Hussein's actions in Iraq.

- Iran, with North Korean assistance, has produced long-range missiles that are capable of reaching Israel and Cyprus and unchecked could quite easily reach Western Europe and America.

- Given Iran's WMD and ballistic missile programmes and its support for terrorism, it is clear that it is not only a threat to regional, but also to world security.

- If Iran, like Libya, has been influenced by the Iraq war into truly reforming, then we must welcome that. However, given Iran's past hostility and its human rights record we must proceed with extreme caution, as indeed we must with all other rogue states.

- A nuclear-armed Iran would be extremely dangerous and, as President George W Bush made clear, must never be allowed to happen.

- If it became clear that Iran was nuclear armed or was on the verge of becoming so, and was planning to attack us or our interests or allies, or if it actually did, we must not be afraid to disarm Iran and remove the Ayatollah from power by force.

- It is in our interests, both economically and security-wise, to encourage states to be free and democratic.

- A free and democratic country is much less likely to be a security risk as it is far less likely to have a government, especially a dictatorship, with a hatred of the West.

- Free and democratic countries are far more likely to trade with the West and therefore be of economic value to the West and themselves.

- We must stand firm against rogue states, as they would damage our freedom, just as the terrorists that they support would.

- Sometimes to protect ourselves we must stop a rogue state from attacking (whether themselves or via terrorism) by using pre-emptive action.

- It is no use waiting until an attack (carried out by whatever means) happens, for then people (and therefore their freedom) will have been harmed. Pre-emptive action prevents this from happening and, as the saying goes, prevention is better than cure.

- Stopping a rogue regime not only protects us, but it also gives people freedom and that is the most important point to remember when dealing with rogue states.

- The most important victory that is won when a rogue regime is removed is that the people of that country are given for the first time the most important right of all: freedom.

Chapter 6

DEALING WITH POTENTIAL ROGUE STATES

Introduction

The last chapter covered rogue states, 'rogue states' in the sense that they are all a direct threat to our security. As the last chapter was concerned with states hostile to us and that are, as I have tried to prove, a direct threat to us, this chapter is concerned with other countries that, whilst not being direct threats to our security, still present issues which need to be discussed. All these countries have important issues surrounding them, from cycles of terrorism to corrupt, oppressive governments. They have been selected because they fit in with the overall theme of this book: freedom and democracy are the right of all and capitalism, not communism, will ultimately be victorious and will allow the freedom of all to be advanced.

Rogues of the Future

But before we examine individual states and their issues, we need first to look to the future, indeed to states that may not exist as of yet. It is theoretically possible for any state to become a rogue state, although there are, in practice, those that are far more likely to become rogue states than others. The first thing that should alert us to the likelihood of a state becoming a rogue state is that it is being governed by an oppressive, totalitarian, undemocratic regime. Undemocratic states are far more likely to become rogue states for the simple reason that they are far more likely to be ruled by a doctrine dictatorship that may well have anti-Western beliefs (as have Iran and North Korea). A democratic country is far less likely to have such a government, as people tend to choose governments that will do the best by them, and this rarely includes spending goodly portions of taxpayers' money on WMD programmes that could lead to a nuclear war with the West. The simple point is that democratic governments are less likely to be extreme (and, for the purposes of this chapter anti-Western) as a democratic government represents (or at least should represent) the majority rather than the minority that is usually represented by the extremists.

The second thing that should alert us to the fact that a state is a rogue of the future, is when it is in the middle of, or on the brink of, a civil war or any other form of revolution or coup d'état. Of course, that is not say that all coups or uprisings are a bad thing. For, if the people in an oppressed country (which may well be a modern day rogue state) rise up to overthrow an oppressive regime (as recently happened in Georgia and Haiti), we should support them. Not only are the people of that country given freedom, but also the world is rid of one more rogue state. After an oppressive regime is overthrown in this way then it is the duty of the free world to aid that country in rebuilding itself so that, in time, it can become a free and democratic nation.

But in countries where the civil war or revolution or coup or whatever other name such an uprising might go by, is being waged against a democratic or reformist regime then we must be on our guard, for, if the uprising is successful, then an oppressive, extreme, anti-Western regime may come into power. This is exactly what happened in Iran when the Ayatollah Khomeini overthrew the Shah. The Shah's regime might not have been the freest or the most democratic one in the world, but it was at least making the necessary reforms to Iran's (or Persia, as it was then) democracy (indeed, the speed and the wide range of the Shah's reforms may have been his downfall). In addition, the Shah's regime was far freer and far less dangerous than the one which replaced it.

To stop such a dangerous regime as the Ayatollah's coming to power in similar circumstances, the international community should support (physically, rather than just 'morally') the side that would pose the least danger to us (which would probably be the more democratically inclined and reformist side). The argument, 'We shouldn't interfere because it is not our business', should hold no sway, as, if the regime that takes over is hostile and willing to attack us (as are Iran and North Korea), then it most certainly does become our business. So, therefore, it is our business to support the most pro-Western side, even if it is not entirely democratic or free, as chances are that it holds our values – such as freedom – in high regard and is therefore more likely to reform than an anti-Western regime. People must accept that even if we are not entirely happy with it, it is far better to support a not entirely tasteful pro-Western regime to stop a far more distasteful regime that is likely to be downright hostile to us, taking power. It is truly a case of 'better the devil you know'.

The third point that should warn us that a state is potentially a rogue state is if the regime is politically unstable. If a regime (again, most likely a dictatorship) is on the brink of collapse, it may well be inclined to launch an attack on us in an attempt to regain the popular support of its people. Such an attack could even be an invasion of a disputed territory. Indeed this is exactly what happened in 1982 when Argentina invaded the Falkland Islands. The political instability of the ruling Argentine military junta under General Leopold Galtieri (shortly after the Falklands War, Galtieri fell from power) led to the war of aggression against British territory and British subjects.

Any politically unstable regime might launch such an attack if it thought that it would prevent its fall. That is why we must always be aware of such regimes that most certainly have the potential to be rogue states (indeed many current rogue states are politically unstable) for these are probably the most dangerous states of all.

Rogue states can seemingly just 'appear', but in many cases there are some warning signs. The main three warning signs are:

- Undemocratic, often oppressive, and totalitarian regimes that are run by doctrine dictatorships or similar ruling elites.

- Countries in or on the brink of civil war in which one of the parties involved is likely to instate an extreme, oppressive, anti-Western regime (as happened in Iran).

- Politically unstable regimes that may, above all other rogues, be inclined to launch an attack against a country as a means of gaining popular support so as to bolster the regime.

But being able to identify which states are the rogues of the future is just half of the problem. Simply identifying these states will not stop them becoming rogue states. If in the 'rogue state of the future' there is a rebel group that is fighting against the regime, the free world must give aid and support to that group, provided they were willing, if the ruling regime were finally defeated, to allow freedom and democracy to come to that country. However, if any such rebel organisation were to lead to another anti-Western, rogue regime then, of course, we should give them no support, but instead treat that country as if it were a potential rogue state anyway.

If a country is a 'rogue of the future', then we should make it openly known that we dislike the way that the country is heading and that we are not afraid of dealing with it in the manner in which we have dealt with rogue states in the past – whether that be through heavy sanctions or the actual removal of the regime. In addition to this we should make our support known for any moderate or reformist opinion, especially if held by people with some sway.

The final option open to us when dealing with a 'rogue of the future' is to actually impose economic sanctions. Such sanctions would obviously not be as harsh as they would be if that state were already a rogue state, but may well shock such a state into turning away from the path to becoming a rogue state. Economic sanctions would naturally be the final recourse against a 'rogue of the future' as other options, that are less damaging, would be desirable.

The above option would clearly only be useful in the case of 'rogues of the future' that fell into the categories of 'undemocratic regime with the potential to become extreme' or 'politically unstable regime'. If a state was likely to become a 'rogue of the future' because the ruling, pro-Western regime was to be overthrown in a coup, then the above action would quite clearly do more harm than good. In such a scenario, as I have said earlier, we should give aid and support to the regime or to the pro-Western and suitably democratic side in the conflict, so as to stop a dangerous regime remaining in, or coming to power. And that is ultimately the most important point to remember when dealing with potential rogue states – we must stop dangerous regimes taking power.

The Holy Land

Of all the conflicts in the world, the one that keeps going and often seems to be irresolvable is the Israeli–Palestinian conflict. As with most international disputes, the cause is predominately land, but again, as in many conflicts, religion also plays an important part. What we now know as Israel has for centuries been a flashpoint, given that it has within it – indeed, within Jerusalem itself – extremely important sites (in two cases, the most important sites) for three major religions: Christianity, Islam and Judaism. In the Middle Ages, the crusaders travelled to Jerusalem and took part in a series of bloody wars as an absolution of all their sins, but now conflict in the Holy Land is essentially over the desire – on the part of both Arabs and Israelis – to live in freedom. The Israelis desire freedom from the threat of terrorism; the Palestinians desire to have the freedom to rule themselves, in their own state, free from occupation. Both sides have equally strong arguments for their respective rights to live on the land, and that is really the key point to bear in mind when dealing with the Israeli–Palestinian conflict: both have equal rights to live on the land and equal arguments in their respective calls for the cessation of occupation and of terrorism.

The origins of the Israeli–Palestinian conflict lie with the division of the former British Mandate of Palestine by the United Nations (UN). The UN divided the area into Arab and Jewish states. However, the land was not divided equally between the two states, the Arab state receiving 44 per cent of the land and the Jewish state receiving 56 per cent of the land. This division was rejected by the Palestinians, which led to a series of Arab–Israeli wars, which drew in several surrounding countries and eventually led to the Israeli occupation of 75 per cent of the land of the former British Mandate of Palestine.

The first of these Arab–Israeli wars started on the day after the state of Israel was declared on 15 May 1948. On that day, five armies from Jordan, Egypt, Lebanon, Syria, and Iraq invaded Israel. However, these armies were repulsed by Israeli forces and when an armistice was called, Israel's borders contained all but 25 per cent of the former Mandate of Palestine. The Egyptian and Jordanian forces retained this land, which was in what are now the West Bank (Jordan) and the Gaza Strip (Egypt). This continued occupation no doubt added to tensions which triggered the next Arab–Israeli War nearly twenty years later.

During this time, the Palestinian Liberation Organisation was set up along with the then secret Fatah movement, both of which were to fall under the leadership of one of the most infamous characters of the Israeli–Palestinian conflict – Yasser Arafat. The second of the Arab–Israeli wars started on 5 June 1967 and has become known for its length or rather lack of it. More commonly known as the Six Day War, this war was to change the face of the Middle East conflict. In the six days of hostilities, Israeli forces seized the Gaza Strip and the Sinai from Egypt and the Golan Heights from Syria, and pushed Jordanian forces out of the West Bank and East Jerusalem, which they had taken some nineteen years before. Despite the fact that Israeli forces had retaken all of the land of the former British Mandate of Palestine (indeed, more, given the Israeli occupation of the Sinai and the Golan Heights), this war, like the first Arab–Israeli War, simply caused another.

The third Arab–Israeli War – indeed, the last in the sense of Arab armies going to war with Israeli armies – occurred in 1973 on the Jewish festival of the Day of Atonement, and it is to this festival's name that the war owes its name – the Yom Kippur War. This war, as I have said above, had its roots in the Six Day War, as it started when Egypt and Syria launched a major offensive against Israel to retake the Sinai and the Golan Heights, which they had been unable to regain by diplomatic means after losing them in the Six Days War. It is, at this point, interesting to note that all the Arab–Israeli wars were started (though not necessarily caused) by

Arab forces launching an attack on Israel. The significance of this and the cause of the Arab–Israeli wars will be discussed later in this section. In the Yom Kippur War the Egyptians and Syrians, after initial gains in the Sinai and the Golan Heights, were pushed back by Israeli forces, which eventually even took land beyond the armistice line of the Six Day War, although these gains, in Syria at least, were later given up. The end of this war only came about with diplomatic interventions from the USA, the Soviet Union, and the UN.

The main result of this war, indeed a result that has stayed with the Middle East peace process ever since, was that Israel became more reliant on the USA for military, diplomatic and economic support. The other major result of this war was that Saudi Arabia led a petrol embargo against Israel's supporters. This embargo caused worldwide fuel shortages and a sharp rise in petrol prices across the world. This embargo, which lasted until March 1974, and the fuel shortages and price rises that went with it just go to show that the Arab–Israeli conflict affects the entire world – not just Arabs and Israelis.

The significance of the Arab–Israeli conflict means that it is the business of the entire world and therefore its peaceful settlement is in the interests of the entire world. But before we look at ways in which the conflict could be solved and what this would mean for the region and the world as a whole, we must look at its most recent history and the views and beliefs that each side holds which leads them to take the action that they do.

The next major step in the Arab–Israeli conflict after the Yom Kippur War of 1973 was when President Anwar Sadat of Egypt became the first Arab leader to recognise Israel, when he flew to Israel and addressed the Israeli Parliament on 10 November 1977. This action led to the signing, by Egypt and Israel, of the Camp David Accords in 1978, which set out a framework for peace in the Middle East, including some autonomy for the Palestinians. In 1979, Israeli Prime Minister Menachem Begin and President Sadat of Egypt signed a bilateral Egyptian–Israeli peace treaty that led to Israel returning the Sinai – which had originally been occupied some twelve years earlier – to Egypt. As well as taking steps to make the Middle East more peaceful, these actions on the part of President Sadat, led to other Arab states boycotting Egypt for 'breaking ranks' and ultimately led to President Sadat being assassinated by Islamist elements of the Egyptian army in 1981.

In 1987 the first intifada or mass uprising of Palestinian people against the Israeli occupation of the West Bank and the Gaza Strip occurred and led, by its end in 1993, to the deaths of over 1,000 Palestinian civilians. Around this time (1993), a major step was taken in resolving the Israeli–Palestinian conflict. Israeli Prime Minister Yitzhak Rabin, and Foreign Minister Simon Peres and his deputy, Yossi Beilin, initiated talks with the Palestinians in Norway, which led to the Declaration of Principles that were signed on the White House lawns and sealed with the historic handshake between Yitzhak Rabin and Yasser Arafat.

The first year of Palestinian self-rule in Jericho and Gaza led to bombings by Palestinian extremists, and Israeli blockades and the assassination of Palestinian militants. A second round of peace talks was met with little enthusiasm by the Palestinians, while the Israeli religious right was furious at what it saw as the surrender of Jewish land. This culminated, on 4 November 1995, with the assassination of Prime Minister Rabin by a Jewish religious extremist. As with the assassination of the other person who looked likely to bring peace to the Middle East, President Sadat, Yitzhak Rabin's assassination showed that there are always those willing to stop peace. We must never allow them to win, for if they do, peace can never come to the Middle East.

After Yitzhak Rabin's assassination, peace efforts broke down and a succession of Israeli prime ministers have made little impact. Increasing numbers of terrorist attacks on Israel – predominately suicide bombings – have led to more Israeli incursions into the West Bank and Gaza Strip and to several assassinations of Palestinian extremists and even of the leader of the terrorist group Hamas, Sheik Yassin Ahmed. These acts have led in turn to more suicide bombings, which provoke more Israeli incursions and so on. This cycle of bloodshed, which has gone on now for many years, clearly must be ended, but this goal is difficult to achieve as both the Israelis and the Palestinians have suffered at each other's hands and each side sees the other to be in the wrong. And the situation is made no easier to resolve by the fact that both sides are at least partially right in the claims that they make against each other. As I have said earlier, the one thing that must be remembered is that both sides are correct in their claims to the right to live upon the land. Both Israelis and Palestinians have this right and that is the key point to bear in mind when considering the Israeli–Palestinian conflict.

It is clear that the conflict cannot be resolved through the means employed by the Israelis and the Palestinians in recent years: in the case of the Palestinians, terrorist attacks and, in the case of the Israelis, military incursions and assassinations. At this point, however, it is worth noting that those who are behind and those who support terrorist acts are probably in the minority, whilst the majority are those who want to live in peace, freedom and with security, without the bloodshed of recent years. Those behind the acts of terror are rarely those who represent the majority, but the militant minority who are really out for their own personal gain.

To me, the most sensible and logical way for the Israeli–Palestinian conflict to be resolved is for both sides to stop their activities and, after a set period of time where neither side commits acts of violence against each other, a Palestinian state be formed. For such a state to work the authorities there would have to take a very tough stance on terrorism, which, after all, is a crime, and the people who carry out and plan acts of terrorism are therefore criminals. The government of such a Palestinian state would have to be willing to clamp down on terrorists and other such extremists and to cooperate with Israel, for not only would Israel and a new Palestinian state border each other, but a fledgling Palestinian state would, for a while at least, be very poor, so would be reliant on aid which would have to come from, or at least through Israel or Jordan. What would not be acceptable would be a Palestinian government made up of extremists who were set against Israel. But such a government would probably not be elected by the Palestinian people as they would have seen that peace, not violence, got them their country and they would be unwilling to lose through violence what they had gained through peace.

One of the main points of contention when there is talk of a Palestinian state is that of Jerusalem. Jerusalem has been a flashpoint since the crusades and continues to be so quite simply because three major world religions have their most important sites there as mentioned earlier. Each religion can lay claim to Jerusalem in some way, and has. That is why it is quite clear that neither side can have Jerusalem within their territory, or have full sovereignty over it.

The most logical way to solve the problem as regards the control of access to Jerusalem would be for both the Israelis and the Palestinians to have sovereignty over Jerusalem in some joint sovereignty agreement or for Jerusalem to be ruled by some neutral authority (for example, the UN), which would allow open access to the city by both sides. Given the Israelis' and Palestinians' quite understandable mistrust of each other, a neutral Jerusalem would probably be the best option. It would be run by an international force of peacekeepers, so as to allow equal and open access to both the Israelis and Palestinians. Of course entry to such a neutral Jerusalem would have to be controlled along the lines of an international land border so as to prevent those intent on harming the peace from doing so. The only problem with the idea of a neutral Jerusalem is what to do with the (predominately Israeli) population already living there. Of course, moving people out of Jerusalem, if it became neutral, would naturally be completely out of the question. Not only would this make Jerusalem a ghost town, but it would be repeating what has happened to the people of that region for the last two millennia. The best, indeed the only, answer to this problem is quite simple: allow people to go on living there (of course, only if they wished to do so) under the neutral authority, with the right to free access to the rest of their country.

The other main point of contention in any peace plan are the Israeli settlements in the West Bank and the Gaza Strip. Whilst these settlements are on Palestinian land and are seen by many Palestinian groups to be the ultimate symbol of Israeli power in the area, it should be remembered that they are people's homes. To throw them out just because some peace deal says so seems to go against the principle that people should be able to live, within reason, where they choose. Also, and perhaps more importantly, removing the Israeli settlements would add to the feeling that the

Israelis and Palestinians should, for some reason, not live on the same land as each other. In other words removing the Israeli settlements and settlers therein would, at best, help to maintain the gulf that has kept the two peoples at war for so long, or, at worst, it would actually add to such a culture. The 'us and them' ideas of some Israelis and Palestinians alike do not help the peace process; indeed, they may actually hinder it.

The best thing to do with the Israeli settlements would probably be to leave them and to allow the settlers to stay if they wished. Removing all the Israeli settlements and sending all the settlers back to Israel would, as I have said earlier, just make the division worse. That would not be a desirable thing either for Israel or for a newly formed Palestinian state, as, again as I have said earlier, any divisions between the two states, either physical (i.e. the 'security' wall) or mental, leads to both sides being set against each other. This, in turn, leads to yet another cycle of violence. Both Israelis and Palestinians make it explicitly clear in their respective declarations of independence[31] that they are willing to accept people of any race or religion living within their territory. The declarations also show the feelings of both sides, and therefore the difficulties that have to be overcome. Indeed some settlers remaining after a Palestinian state was set up (the settlements and settlers would, of course, be under Palestinian jurisdiction) would make an extremely strong link between the two states, which would help to establish mutual cooperation.

The Israeli–Palestinian conflict will only be resolved on the basis of mutual cooperation. Both the Israelis and the Palestinians have perfectly equal rights to live on the land and equally they must accept that compromises and concessions will have to be made if they are to peacefully co-exist. The following is what seems to me to be the best plan for securing peace in the area:

1   Both Israelis and the Palestinians refrain from violent action against each other for a set period of time (say, six

---

[31] See the Israeli Declaration of Independence, 14 May 1948
<http://yale.edu/lawweb/avalon/mideast/israel.htm>
and the Palestinian Declaration of Independence, 15 November 1988
<http://www.palestine-net.com/politics/indep.html>

months) – this includes acts of terrorism and the assassination of militants.

2 If the above is complied with, then a Palestinian state should be set up with the condition that it is free and democratic and does not support terrorism. This means that it would have to bring to justice the terrorists who are responsible for previous terrorist attacks against Israel.

3 A Jerusalem with shared sovereignty – or, better still, a neutral Jerusalem accessible to both Israelis and Palestinians – be set up so that neither side is in control of the city that is at the heart of the cultures of so many different people, not just Israeli and Palestinian.

4 Current Israeli settlements to come under the jurisdiction of the new Palestinian state, but settlers be allowed to remain if they wished so as to help to forge links between Israel and the Palestinian state which would be essential for any Palestinian state to succeed.

This plan, for it to be a success, requires high levels of cooperation between the Israelis and Palestinians and the international community. A high level of cooperation between Israel and Palestine would, in itself, be useful, as it would help to build the bonds between the two peoples that are essential if peace is to be achieved. The Palestinian authorities would have to bring terrorists to justice and prevent further acts of terror, which only serve to inflame the tensions in the area. On the Israeli side, they would have to cease activities such as the assassination of terrorist group leaders who really should be brought to face justice in the same manner as any other criminal. On the Israeli part as well, it would mean removing the security barrier, which, whilst being a perfectly understandable measure, just goes to cause more resentment on the Palestinian side. Indeed, the removal of the security barrier could be a step taken at a certain stage within the period of non-violence, as a sign that Israel was willing to cooperate.

The key to resolving the Israeli–Palestinian conflict is for both sides to accept that they both have equal rights to live on the land.

The other point that must be accepted by the Israelis and the Palestinians is that they have both carried out acts that were wrong and provoked more violence. In the case of the Israelis this means accepting that their prolonged occupation of the Sinai and the Golan Heights led to the 1973 Yom Kippur War and that the assassination of Palestinian militants (who should have been brought to justice rather than being assassinated) and other such acts lead to more terrorist attacks against them. However, that is not to say that Israel should give up in the face of terrorism (as, indeed, nobody should) and that is why, therefore, the Palestinians must be willing to accept that terrorists and those who have masterminded terrorist attacks are not freedom fighters, as they claim, but criminals who need to be brought to justice. If both sides do not openly accept these points then resentment or ill feelings will remain on both sides and, if such sentiment remains, peace can never come to Israel and Palestine.

If peace is to be achieved, much cooperation will be needed on both sides. In the early days of any state there are always problems, so it would be folly to expect anything less in the early days of a Palestinian state. A newly formed Palestinian state would need Israel's cooperation if it were to be successful. That is one of the major points of the issue. Personally, I believe that both the Israelis and the Palestinians have the will to bring peace to the area. Both of their respective declarations of independence show that they are willing to accept each other and this is what both sides must do to bring about peace; accept each other's right to live there. Only through cooperation with, and this acceptance of each other can peace be brought to them.

Zimbabwe

Those who are in any doubt that state controls and consciously directed plans to redistribute wealth cause oppression should look at Zimbabwe. President Robert Mugabe has had a policy, since he and his Zanu-PF party came to power in 1980, of redistributing white-owned farmland to the majority black population of his country. He and his party's reason for doing this is that land, which is now owned by white farmers, was unlawfully taken from the native population of Zimbabwe when British colonial forces mandated Zimbabwe (then called Rhodesia). Therefore Mugabe has ordered that white-owned farmland is to be redistributed amongst the black population of Zimbabwe. However, in real terms this means that land is given to Mugabe's Cabinet, supporters, and party members. Recently the worsening economic crisis there has brought Zimbabwe to the brink of famine. This crisis has not been helped by Mugabe's latest election victory, which many commentators have denounced as being rigged. Zimbabwe is really the ultimate contemporary example of what happens when a government implements a consciously directed plan for the redistribution of land and wealth.

Mugabe's land redistribution and his other economic controls are the first points to look at when considering Zimbabwe. The rights and wrongs of history and, moreover, British colonial rule could be debated for hours, but surely the aim of any government is to ensure fairness and equality of opportunity for all its people, whatever their race or creed. Mugabe's land redistribution scheme, however attractive it may sound to some, clearly benefits neither black nor white Zimbabweans. When land is seized, not only does it cease to be as productive as it was (or in some cases not productive at all), but it is given to Mugabe's supporters in the Zanu-PF party. This corruption, of course, only benefits Mugabe's supporters; all others – not least his political opponents – are left with no benefit from the land whatsoever.

Zimbabwe is a predominately agricultural nation, so obviously most people rely on the land to make a living. However, since farms have been seized, unemployment has risen to the 60 per cent mark and over 5 million people are in need of food aid. This humanitarian crisis occurred because the people have no money, as they have no work. These huge levels of unemployment have been brought about by Mugabe's policy of returning Zimbabwe to what are barely subsistence levels of agricultural production and, moreover, by his policy of having a centrally directed economy with state enterprise only – in other words, socialism.

Mugabe's policy of seizing white-owned land, which is quite simply a natural progression of the socialist state, has exacerbated, if not caused, the employment and therefore food problems faced by Zimbabwe. Many black Zimbabweans, who are supposed to be the beneficiaries of Mugabe's land redistribution policy, have not been able to work since the white-owned farms they worked on were seized by the 'war veterans' – the self-styled Zanu-PF party militia. These people, on Mugabe's orders, stop workers from working and therefore earning money, which, in turn, adds to the food problem. The 'war veterans' guard the farms for their new tenants who often have no background in farming. Mugabe's policies of state controls and land redistribution, and the terrible suffering that has occurred amongst ordinary Zimbabweans as a result of these policies proves that socialism leads to the oppression of peoples' freedom. Mugabe's absolute corruption (which is blatantly obvious when it comes to the redistribution of land) and his seemingly absolute power go to prove correct Lord Acton's comment (commonly quoted in criticism of socialist and communist leaders), 'Power tends to corrupt; absolute power corrupts absolutely.'

Indeed, as with virtually every country that has had a fully-fledged socialist government that has embarked on a policy of land redistribution and the like, Zimbabwe has a ruler with all but absolute power. Despite the guise of democracy seen in the last elections in Zimbabwe, it became clear to all but the most short-sighted (or biased) of international observers that the election had been, in some way, rigged. In Robert Mugabe's Zimbabwe, however, vote rigging took on a far more sinister form than simple vote fixing. Supporters and officials from the opposition party, the Movement for Democratic Change (MDC), were attacked, generally harassed, abducted, threatened, and even arrested on charges of treason. Indeed, the leader of the MDC, Morgan Tsvangirai, is on trial for treason, facing the possibility of the death penalty.

Such intimidation and oppression of political parties show that Robert Mugabe, even if he was once democratically elected president of Zimbabwe, is now just another common or garden dictator. As with all dictators, Mugabe is obsessed, positively paranoid, about his own power. So, following in a great dictatorial tradition, Mugabe has redefined the word 'treason' and passed other laws to include (to quote from his Public Order and

Security Act (POSA)) anything which causes: 'hatred, contempt or ridicule of the President'.[32] Such laws sound like something out of the Soviet Union under Josef Stalin, but that is hardly surprising – both Mugabe and Stalin (or Dzhugashvili, to give him is real name) are paranoid socialist dictators with only one real concern: their own power.

If any more evidence is required to prove that Mugabe is a typical, undemocratic and ruthless dictator, one only has to look to the food crisis in Zimbabwe. Again, following in the traditions of past dictators, Robert Mugabe has politicised the food that his country receives. Despite the fact that around half his population face starvation, for people to receive food aid, they must produce a Zanu-PF party membership card. Any opposition supporters who dare queue for food are told to 'get their food from Tony Blair'.[33] This politicisation of food aid is yet another throwback to old socialist doctrine, in particular Leon Trotsky's 'who does not obey shall not eat' statement of 1937[34] and therefore shows in no uncertain terms just what kind of government Robert Mugabe runs.

Given the fact that his regime has caused such damage to Zimbabwe's economy (for example, the production of tobacco, one of Zimbabwe's most important cash crops, has fallen by at least 10 per cent) it is likely that the regime will not be able to function and will eventually collapse. However, past experience with countries in similar economic situations shows that the collapse of a regime through economic reasons can be a very slow process, where the situation gets far worse before it improves. In Zimbabwe the situation cannot afford to get much worse given that so many people there are already on the brink of starvation. So, if we left Mugabe's regime to collapse of its own accord a terrible humanitarian disaster would ensue. It is clear that the international community must do something about Zimbabwe.

What we must do, and thankfully is already being done, at

---

[32] Zimbabwean Public Order and Security Act, quoted in Amnesty International's *Report 2003*, < http://web.amnesty.org/report2003/zwe-summary-eng>

[33] Joseph Winter, 'Mugabe outfoxes his critics', *BBC News Online*, 10 February 2003, <http://news.bbc.co.uk/1/hi/world/africa/2744849.stm>

[34] See p.11.

least to an extent, is to make it clear to Mugabe and his regime that its human rights abuses (that includes the politicisation of food aid and vote rigging) are unacceptable and that the international community is not willing to stand by and let them happen. To make this point to Mugabe, we must withdraw international cooperation by cutting links (such as the Commonwealth, which has, of course, already been done) and by pulling out of international events, such as the cricket World Cup.

The cricket World Cup is probably the latest reason why Mugabe and Zimbabwe have been brought to international attention, moreover British attention. The vacillation that has occurred over whether the England cricket team should go to Zimbabwe makes our position look weak, which is something to be avoided when dealing with states such as Mugabe's Zimbabwe. This particular issue has not been helped by former foreign secretary Jack Straw's comments that the England cricket team might have to go to Zimbabwe or English cricket may be 'irrecoverably damaged'. Not only does this statement make the British position look even weaker and to an extent divided, but it also shows that Mr Straw should get his priorities right, for if he thinks that cricket is more important than human rights – as he appears to do from his statement – then he should not have been foreign secretary.

The issue of the cricket World Cup poses the first question of what we should do (or now, what we should have done) as regards Zimbabwe. With regard to the question of whether the England cricket team should have gone to Zimbabwe, the answer is quite simple; they should not. The team going to Zimbabwe will have sent the message to Mugabe and the rest of the world that we thought everything (that is, within Zimbabwe) was normal and that we accepted what Mugabe was, human rights abuses and all. It is clear that we should not send such messages to such states, as this only encourages others. Therefore, the England cricket team should not have gone to Zimbabwe, because this will have effectively sent a green card from us for Mugabe to carry on as he is currently doing. Whatever damage might have been done to English cricket, we must remember that an entire people's freedom is far more important than cricket.

Secondly, we must ask what we can do to stop Mugabe's regime continuing its succession of human rights abuses. The obvious answer is to impose economic sanctions against Zimbabwe. However, with such a high proportion of Zimbabwe's population living so close to the starvation line, such sanctions (if combined with Mugabe's politicisation of food aid) would have the potential to make the situation in Zimbabwe much, much worse before they made it any better. Anyway, the ultimate aim of any economic sanction is to cause damage to a country's economy (and therefore, in theory at least, to make it listen and change its policies), but as Robert Mugabe is already doing such a good job of ruining his country's economy, it seems almost pointless for the international community to help him do so. Having said that, economic sanctions that specifically target the most corrupt of Zimbabwe's industries (of which there are plenty) and therefore cause the most damage to Mugabe and his regime, rather than ordinary Zimbabweans, would be useful, as they would help to hasten the collapse of Mugabe and his Zanu-PF regime, which is ultimately the best thing that can happen for the people of Zimbabwe.

Despite what Mugabe and selected others may argue, the Zanu-PF's regime is not democratic. The last election was clearly unfair and, as elections are one of the most important expressions of freedom and democracy, any country stopping fair elections is undemocratic. To hasten Mugabe's collapse, we must isolate him and his regime and stop its sources of funding wherever possible. By isolating Mugabe, there is a remote chance that he might make some movement towards democratic change, as he may realise that he cannot function without international cooperation. (This is highly unlikely, as he seems set on his current course. Of course, any insanity on Mugabe's part is as for Colonel Gaddafi and Kim Jong-il: it hardly matters, since Mugabe is in power, mad or not.)

If by some miracle Mugabe does realise the error of his ways as it were, then as a sign that he was truly committed to democratic change and was, most importantly, willing to allow the people of Zimbabwe the chance to have true freedom, Mugabe should hold fair, unbiased elections, free from any violence or intimidation intended to 'sway' the electorate. Any such election should take place under international supervision and, if necessary, in the presence of international peacekeeping troops. In such an election, any party, including Mugabe's, would be allowed to stand, as blocking any party from standing would seem – at least in the eyes of the Zimbabwean electorate who are all too familiar with biased elections – to be making the elections unfair, which is almost on a par with what Mugabe is doing at this present time.

Of course, such reform is hardly likely to occur under Mugabe. There is probably a next to zero chance of any such reform. Therefore, we must ask ourselves what we can do to free the people of Zimbabwe from the terrible oppression in which they live. Simply hoping for a change like that described above is not enough; given Mugabe's past record, we can be almost certain that it will not happen. Experience of similar states shows us that they will not reform unless they have to. The best way to help the people of Zimbabwe to have a brighter, freer tomorrow is by removing Robert Mugabe and his Zanu-PF regime from power and then allowing a free and democratic government to take its place.

To my mind, the best way is to remove the regime's source of power, which in some cases is its army and in others an oppressive KGB-cum-Gestapo style police force. In Mugabe's case, his power does not rest with an 'official' organisation, but with his party militia/mob – the self-styled war veterans. If there is any doubt that this mob does Mugabe's bidding, one only has to look at which group has seized the most farmland and which group was responsible for the most politically motivated violence within Zimbabwe during the recent election campaigns. So, it is clear that this mob or militia, or whatever other name they happen to go by, is Mugabe's main tool of oppression and therefore the main way by which he remains in power. The best way to topple Mugabe and to give liberty to the people of Zimbabwe is to remove this militia or at least make it so that they do not support Mugabe.

Of course the removal of the militia Mugabe uses to stay in power is easier said than done. If the militia has any international sources of funding, which chances are will be the same as the Zanu-PF party's, then economic restrictions should be placed on those organisations that directly fund the Zanu-PF party,

Mugabe's militia or any other associated 'enterprise'. Also Mugabe's militia could be further weakened if all international aid was distributed by representatives of the aid organisation sending it, so that aid could not be politicised and so that the militia could be further weakened by keeping aid to its members at a minimum. In addition to this, internationally isolating Mugabe may help to weaken his hold on power and therefore his hold on the militia, which would help to bring about the end of his regime. Once Mugabe's regime collapses – and there can be no doubt that it will collapse one day – Zimbabwe will need international assistance if she is to become a free, democratic state. Once Mugabe is gone and the worst of the humanitarian crisis in Zimbabwe is over, open elections, similar to those described above, will have to take place. Zimbabwe will then be able to go freely forward in what will be a far brighter tomorrow than it ever had under Mugabe.

Robert Mugabe has only been able to remain in power for so long, despite his evil ways, because he (very wisely) preys on the West's (moreover Britain's) guilty conscience – the fact that that the West blames itself for the poverty and the way land is distributed in Zimbabwe and the Third World as a whole. As I pointed out in Chapter 4, this is not true, although we are to blame for one thing in Zimbabwe and that is socialism. By exporting socialism to Zimbabwe and the Third World in general, we have helped to create the problems that we see today. As Robert Mugabe is an extreme socialist – he has made this quite clear in his rantings and ramblings about the redistribution of land and wealth – we can be assured that his regime will one day collapse, as all such socialist regimes do eventually, and then the people of Zimbabwe will be able to have true democracy.

To try to balance out the rights and wrongs of history in Zimbabwe (and elsewhere for that matter) will only lead to more suffering amongst the usual victims – the ordinary Zimbabwean people. The government of Zimbabwe that replaces Robert Mugabe's must bear this point in mind, for only when a government looks to the future, and not to the past, can progress be made and real freedom achieved.

Conclusions

- The likeliest rogue states of the future are states that are totalitarian and undemocratic.

- States that are in the middle of or on the brink of civil war are also likely rogue states of the future.

- Uprisings or coups are not necessarily bad. If they are aimed against an existing oppressive regime then we should support the side fighting for freedom, and help establish a free and democratic country.

- We should physically support regimes that are led by pro-Western and pro-democratic reformists who are faced with an uprising of a group that might lead to an extreme, oppressive rogue state, as happened in Iran.

- It may be necessary to support regimes that are not entirely desirable (such as the Shah of Persia) to stop an anti-Western, totalitarian regime (such as the Ayatollah's of Iran) taking power.

- Such regimes will be pro-Western so they are likely to allow democratic change, especially with the influence that we would gain due to our support.

- When dealing with such delicate matters the saying 'better the devil you know' is often worth remembering – just look at Iran. An extreme regime may launch an attack on the West or on our interests in order to gain local public popularity to stay in power, as happened in 1982 with the Falklands War.

- Simply identifying the rogues of the future is not enough. We must stop them becoming rogue states.

- If there is a rebel group fighting for freedom and democracy in such a state then we should support them.

- If there is no such group we should openly support any moderate opinion within that country.

- The threat of or actual use of economic sanctions may pull a potential rogue state away from the brink of becoming an actual rogue state.

- If we are likely to be attacked by such a state or it becomes an actual dangerous rogue state then the use of force may be the only option.

- The Israeli–Palestinian conflict is an age-old conflict that lingers on to this day and will continue to do so if both sides are unwilling to cooperate.

- Israelis and Palestinians have equal rights to live on the land. People should not try to correct the rights and wrongs of history.

- To avoid further conflict in the region, the neutralising of Jerusalem and the allowing of open access to both sides would cut out one of the most contentious issues from the equation.

- If a Palestinian state is created, then Israeli settlements and settlers should be allowed to stay, but under Palestinian jurisdiction.

- Both the Israelis and the Palestinians show that they respect other people and other cultures in their respective declarations of independence. If peace in the region is to be lasting they should both practise what they preach. For a full numbered version of my plan for peace for the area, see p.89.

- Both sides must accept they have both done things that have provoked the other side into response.

- If peace is to come to the area then the terrorists who operate there must be brought to justice.

- Zimbabwe is the prime example of what happens when a state embarks upon a consciously directed economic scheme aimed to redistribute wealth, in particular, land.

- The rights and wrongs of history in Zimbabwe could be endlessly debated, but trying to alter them will only lead

to more suffering for ordinary Zimbabwean people –
black and white.

- Mugabe and his Zanu-PF party are not democratically
  elected – the violence, intimidation, and vote-rigging
  prove that.

- Mugabe, even if he was once the democratically elected
  president, is now an oppressive dictator. His redefining of
  the word treason to include disagreeing with him is proof
  of this.

- Mugabe's politicisation of food aid shows quite clearly
  what type of government he runs.

- We in the West are to blame for only one thing in
  Zimbabwe: we exported socialism there.

- The unemployment crisis that Zimbabwe is currently
  suffering from is thanks to Mugabe's socialist ways.

- We must make it clear to Mugabe and his regime that his
  actions are unacceptable.

- We should cut international links (such as the
  Commonwealth) with Mugabe and make it clear that he
  will remain isolated until he changes.

- The England cricket tour to Zimbabwe should never
  have happened. Not only does it send conflicting messages to Mugabe that can only strengthen him and
  weaken us, it also virtually says to Mugabe that we accept
  what he is doing.

- The England cricket team should not have gone to
  Zimbabwe; those who start talking about the damage that
  such action would have done to English cricket should
  get their priorities right.

- The best way to hasten Mugabe's fall from power is to
  impose economic sanctions against his direct supporter
  and the supporters of his militia.

- Mugabe holds on to his power via his militia, that is, the
  'war veterans' – his mob.

- Mugabe will fall from power as soon as he runs out of money with which to pay the corrupt supporters who keep him in power.

- When this fall comes, or if, by some miracle, Mugabe renounces (genuinely) his old ways in favour of democracy, it is the duty of the free world to ensure that there are open, fair, democratic elections in Zimbabwe so that ordinary Zimbabweans can have the chance to build a free and prosperous future.

Chapter 7
THE FALL OF COMMUNISM

Introduction

During the Cold War, communism was undoubtedly the greatest threat to Western freedom. Even today, communism poses a threat to us, but in the form of the rogue state of North Korea rather than the massed forces of the communism of the past. The threat from North Korea has become the exception rather than the rule. Even though the countries in this chapter are communist – there can, as I will show, be no doubt of that – it has become clear that communism is crumbling away before capitalism in what is now an inexorable (to quote Karl Marx) manner. Indeed, the gradual fall of communism that we are now witnessing could be described as the domino effect in reverse: rather than one country after another falling to communism, one communist country after another is falling to capitalism.

In this chapter I will highlight how three 'major' communist countries are slowly becoming more capitalist and therefore slowly more free. However, I will also show that these countries, Vietnam, Cuba and China are still communist despite what some people, especially on the left, might think. Finally, I will set out what we can do to help these countries break free from the oppressive grip of communism and what the governments of these countries should do in order to bring their people greater freedom and prosperity. Whether the communist roots of the leaders in these countries would actually allow such reforms to go through is another matter entirely. What must be remembered, when considering how all these communist countries have changed and what we and they can (or should) do in order to continue these reforms, is that all communist regimes will eventually fall to capitalism. This is because a country, indeed, a people, will see that free-enterprise capitalism is the only way to make progress and gain greater freedom.

Vietnam

Vietnam is probably one of the best-known communist countries, mainly thanks to the 1964–1975 war in which 58,000 Americans and countless Vietnamese were killed. Despite being one of the places in the world commonly associated with communism, and remembered for US attempts to stop its spread, Vietnam, as with most other communist countries, is gradually becoming 'less' communist and slowly more open to free enterprise and capitalism. The main cause of this decline in communism in Vietnam (as with other communist countries featured within this chapter) is the increased levels of contact these countries now have with capitalist society. Interestingly enough, this point is most clearly illustrated not by any of the countries in this chapter, but by the last redoubt of hardline communism, the most insular and isolated country in the world: North Korea. As North Korean people have virtually no contact with the capitalist world, it remains a haven for hardline communism. On the other hand, countries like Vietnam, which have increased contact with the outside world, mainly through tourism, have become more capitalist.

Communist countries become more capitalist and therefore freer as the ordinary people of the country gain knowledge of the capitalist world and the freedom and opportunities capitalism could bring to them. Tourism to communist countries also plays a big part in bringing down communism, as tourists, ordinary Westerners, are seen by locals, who realise what can be gained through capitalism. Indeed, this is the very reason some communist countries used to (and in some cases, still do) take great zeal in keeping foreigners out so that the people of the communist country would not see what they could have and could achieve if free from the oppressive yoke of communism.

This idea that free-enterprise capitalism brings greater prosperity to a nation has most definitely been realised by the government of Vietnam. As early as 1986, market forces and a degree of free enterprise were introduced to Vietnam's economy and, in 2000, a stock exchange was set up in Vietnam and levels of foreign investment were increased. However, despite this movement towards more market freedom in Vietnam, elements of the ruling Communist Party have become worried – basically because of their fear of losing their grip on power – and there have been several purges on, amongst other things, 'poisonous' CDs, videos and books. (Indeed, there can be no doubt that this book would be considered poisonous by the Vietnamese leadership.)

The main reason for this increased economic liberation is probably because of the tourist industry. The large amounts of money that tourists bring with them will, no doubt, have urged the Vietnamese leadership to become more economically open, so they can benefit from the wealth available through tourism and from contact with other countries in general.

Despite the fact that Vietnam has become more economically open of late, it still has a long way to go before it can truly be considered as having taken to free-enterprise capitalism and therefore individual freedom itself. Vietnam is still ruled by the traditional communist one party system where the 'party' (i.e. the Communist Party) dictates to the entire nation. The country is not truly economically free as its government still owns most property and still consciously directs the economy. The Vietnamese government makes sure that Vietnam trades with socialist and regional countries rather than with countries as dictated by market forces.

Vietnam remains communist; the regime in Hanoi still, despite the progress it has made, restricts people's opportunities according to a preconceived plan. Hanoi still clamps down on anything that it sees as decadent or bourgeois. This shows that Hanoi, like every other communist regime, is paranoid about power and its grip on it. These clampdowns show how the state interferes with everything so as to remain in power, which is a classic hallmark of a communist state. Finally, the fact that Vietnam is still communist is reiterated by Hanoi's use of another classic communist hallmark: its tight grip on all forms of media. Any reports that are deemed 'inaccurate' or 'bad' by the Ministry of Culture – in other words, any report that disagrees with official Communist Party policy – is disallowed and the responsible media group can be shut down. This control of the media – coupled with the fact that ordinary Vietnamese cannot access foreign satellite TV broadcasts and those that are fortunate enough to have access to the Internet can only do so through tight state filtering that blocks sights deemed to be 'reactionary' – shows quite clearly that Hanoi is afraid of its people getting ideas that might make them desire a freer, more democratic country to live in. Even though real progress has been made, it is very true to say that Vietnam is still communist.

Despite this, progress has been made towards making Vietnam more capitalist, which of course brings us closer to the eventual demise of the ruling communist regime in Hanoi, which is, as in all other communist countries, inevitable. However, this does not mean that it will come around quickly – the reverse domino effect is likely to be much slower than its inverse counterpart. In my opinion, communism in Vietnam will not fall as suddenly as it did in East Germany, but it will be eroded gradually by increased capitalist influences being allowed into the Vietnamese economy, and, more importantly, by the increased knowledge of the ordinary Vietnamese people, which will inexorably come with increased contact with capitalist world.

When communism finally does fall in Vietnam – such a fall is likely to come in the form of Hanoi announcing democratic elections – it may not need as much aid and support as one might expect, as the fall of communism there will not be sudden. Vietnam will have built up the means for supporting itself in the capitalist world before communism collapses there. When communism fell in the USSR, even though it had been coming around for a long time, the USSR had very few means with which to support itself within a capitalist society, so the smaller nations of the USSR in particular were reliant on Western aid. However, as Hanoi has introduced free market elements into Vietnam's economy, even a stock exchange, Vietnam has good means with which to support herself. Indeed, the country may require very little economic aid once communism falls there, as she already actively trades in the global market. Countries normally only require economic assistance (in such circumstances) after sudden regime change, which, as I have said earlier, is highly unlikely.

The only assistance that Vietnam may require is independent international observation of the elections that will take place there, and which are all but inevitable after communism finally falls. Any such supervision would be there not because of some incapability on the Vietnamese part to run fair elections, but simply to ensure that the elections were carried out properly. This is often a problem in fledgling democracies, especially those which are converting from dictatorships or one-party systems (as in Vietnam). The best thing that can be done now by those elements of the Vietnamese government who doubtless want to bring about the end of communism is to continue on the path of free enterprise reforms which will bring about the end of communism, albeit gradually, though that, of course, is the best way. As for the rest of the world, all we can do to help bring about the end of communism in Vietnam is to wait and to continue to trade with Vietnam, for trading with such communist countries, far from encouraging communism as it would in countries such as North Korea, will actually help hasten communism's collapse. Contact with capitalism, not military might, is what will now finally defeat all communism in the world.

Cuba

Cuba is another country whose name is synonymous with communism. When Cuba is mentioned, just as with Vietnam, its past is what is best remembered. The piece of Cuban history which is most commonly remembered – a piece of history that indelibly links Cuba with the communism of old – is the Cuban Missile Crisis of 1962. The crisis was probably the closest the Cold War came to becoming the Third World War. It started on 14 October 1962 when reconnaissance photographs from a U2 aircraft confirmed that Soviet ballistic missile sites were in place on Cuba and would shortly be ready for operational use. The fourteen days that followed saw American nuclear forces put on to 'Defcon 2', the alert condition just before actual nuclear deployment and they saw British V-force nuclear bombers placed on Alert Condition 3 – the highest alert condition ever operationally imposed in the history of the British nuclear bomber force.

The situation was only resolved at the eleventh hour by Nikita Khrushchev backing down. This point in history, probably the most dangerous the world has ever seen, is what Cuba is probably best remembered for. Indeed, this incident, which proved Cuba's strategic significance, is what secured Cuba its lifeline of $4–5 billion of subsidies from the USSR every year.

These subsidies allowed Castro and his Communist Party to build up health and education facilities, which were of great repute. However, Castro, as with all communist dictators, decided that he and he alone knew what was best for the Cuban economy. Therefore he failed to diversify it – again another common characteristic of socialist states with consciously directed economies – so, Cuba remained (and to an extent still does remain) reliant on its sugar exports. This lack of diversification continued in the Cuban economy until the USSR fell, and, with its passing, so went the subsidies on which Castro's Cuba depended so much. The disappearance of Soviet subsidies meant that American trade embargoes started to affect Cuba and led to Havana introducing tight rationing of everything from food to energy.

Today, Cuba still retains all the classic elements of a communist state of old. To quote the US State Department, 'Cuba is a totalitarian police state which relies on repressive methods to maintain control.'[35] In other words Castro's government spies on its people and no doubt on its visitors via its secret police (yet another classic hallmark of a totalitarian communist state), the General Directorate for State Security (DGSE). The DGSE intensely surveys, through physical and electronic means, Cuban citizens, and any foreign travellers. Indeed, foreigners in Cuba have very little access to local residents – if any local were to talk to a foreigner they could expect harassment or even detention by the DGSE.[36] This feeling against foreigners and foreign ideas that Castro's government holds is strongest against Americans, their greatest adversaries. However American citizens generally do not have any trouble, simply because they are not allowed to visit Cuba under US law. As well as a ban on its citizens travelling to

---

[35] Consular Information Sheet (Cuba), *US State Department*, 22 May 2006, <http://travel.state.gov/travel/cis_pa_tw/cis/cis_1097.html>

[36] Ibid.

Cuba, the USA has several long-standing trade embargoes on Cuba – which continue even though Castro's regime is desperate for dollars to prop itself up with. This desperation for foreign currency, along with some other factors, has made Castro's Cuba begin to alter its ways to some extent, though this will be dealt with later on in this section.

The other point that proves that Cuba is still a communist country with a long way to go before it can truly make economic progress (that is, when it is free from an oppressive government which consciously directs the economy) is that Havana still keeps a tight grip on the press – in a similar manner to Hanoi – so as to stop any ideas or views which go against government policy being given to the Cuban people. In fact, Havana wishes to control such matters so completely that it is an offence in Cuba, punishable by up to three years imprisonment, to broadcast (in any way) anti-government propaganda or to insult government officials – both ideas which seem ludicrous in free, Western society. This restriction of the press is a classic communist trait, as a free press might encourage ideas deemed unallowable in a state such as Cuba. The severely restricted press in Cuba is clearly another ploy on the part of Castro's government to try to remain in power (for Castro and his government, like all other communist governments, have a huge paranoia about falling from power) by stopping its people from learning what the outside, free capitalist world can offer.

Despite the fact that Cuba is still clearly an oppressive totalitarian state – indeed it is almost on the verge of being ranked alongside states such as Iran and North Korea – it has made some, limited progress towards becoming more economically free (and therefore freer overall) and more capitalist. This change in Havana's policy comes not because of some realisation on their part of the wonders of free-enterprise capitalism, but from what is probably the strongest force within any communist government: the desire to remain in power. As Castro's regime is on the verge of economic collapse, it has become clear to the Cuban leadership that they need money – moreover, US dollars – to keep them afloat. This realisation first became apparent as early as 1993 when US dollars were made legal in Cuba, notably only three years after the Soviet Union fell and took with it its regular payments to Cuba.

In order to gain this money with which to prop itself up, Havana has had to become slightly more economically open. The main way that foreign revenue is brought to Cuba is, as in Vietnam, through tourism. Havana has realised that it can make huge amounts of money by making Cuba more accessible to tourists who seem willing to travel there, given Cuba's comparatively low prices, natural beauty and, to an extent, history. As well as bringing with them much needed revenue for Castro's regime, tourists also carry with them ideas from the Western capitalist world. However hard Havana tries to stop these ideas 'leaking' into the general Cuban population, it is inevitable that they will, and, as happened in East Germany, the people of Cuba will start to want reform and greater freedoms, something that Castro and his regime seem completely opposed to. In Cuba, as in Vietnam, tourism has, and will, play a major part in ending the incumbent communist regimes.

Despite the similarities between their situations, the likely falls of communism in Cuba and Vietnam will be very different from each other. Whereas the fall of communism in Vietnam is likely to be very gradual, the fall of communism in Cuba is likely to be very sudden indeed. There seems to me to be two possibilities for Cuba. The first one of these is for there to be a 'Berlin Wall' style collapse of communism. In this scenario, the fall comes after a period in which Cuba and, more importantly, the ordinary Cubans have increased contact with the capitalist world – that is, through tourism. This scenario would take quite a long time to come about, given the way the Castro government is at present. If it did happen, Cuba would need international assistance so as to rehabilitate herself.

The second and, indeed, the more likely of the two scenarios, is where the years of American sanctions pay off and Castro's regime be replaced either by a popular uprising or some other coup. If this were to happen and the new regime seemed willing to cooperate with the West and was willing for open democracy in Cuba, then we must give that regime the aid and support that it needs.

However, if any regime that succeeds Castro's were anti-Western and undemocratic – for example, if any coup were led by hardline communist elements – then we would have another problem on our hands. If such a regime was very isolationist and was going to pose no real threat to us then we could leave it to fall of its own accord, which it would do a lot more quickly than Castro's regime. If, however, such a new regime started to support rogue regimes intent on damaging the capitalist world (i.e. the USA) – such as North Korea – then we would have a very real threat on our hands. If a state such as North Korea started to support Cuba and vice versa, then it would not take long for such a state to exploit Cuba's strategic value. If such a scenario were to happen we would be faced with a stark choice: either remove such a hardline militant regime from Havana by force or risk what very nearly happened in October 1962 becoming a reality.

China

China is probably the best known of all the current communist states, not because it is communist and has the world's largest population, but because it is the last of potentially hostile nuclear-armed states. Indeed, this is a point the Chinese authorities love to play on, and it also makes some Western countries cautious in their dealings with the People's Republic of China – but it should not. When Beijing starts to use its nuclear arsenal to try to exert its authority over the West, the facts and moreover the figures of the matter should be remembered. China has around eighteen thermonuclear-armed ICBMs that could strike the USA, whereas the USA has 6,000 thermonuclear warheads capable of striking China. Whatever Beijing may claim, it can in no way compete on the nuclear superpower scale.

Of all the communist states in the world, China was among the first to begin economic reform. Even in the early 1980s, China's famous Maoist collective farms began to be dismantled, and private enterprise, for which the Chinese historically have a flair, was allowed again. This new economic liberalisation has allowed living standards in China to go up alongside manufacturing (mainly of electronic goods and clothing). China has recently joined the World Trade Organisation, which will further boost its economy, which has had, on average, 7 per cent growth per year since 1979, given that it will have greater access to foreign markets. This increase in free-enterprise capitalism in China will also help to hasten the demise of the remaining state-owned industries, 75 per cent of which are loss-making.

Despite the huge reforms that China has made as regards economic freedom, it still has a long way to go in the realm of political freedoms. However, as economic and political freedoms are inextricably linked, it is most likely that the latter will follow the former. Indeed, on a local scale some democratic reform is already coming to China. Reasonably democratic elections have taken place at a village level. Although it may not remove the undemocratic ruling Communist Party from power, such quasi-democracy can lead to full democracy as it did in the Soviet Union. In the People's Republic of China it is highly likely that we shall see democracy come about as economic freedoms grow.

Even though China has made many more positive steps towards becoming more democratic and free, there are still problem areas. For a start, whilst living standards have gone up, there are still huge numbers of people living in poverty in the rural areas of China. Of course, a pronounced wealth gap between rural and city workers is common in many industrialising countries, but it shows what China is: an industrialising nation, not some economic superpower, or tiger economy, as Beijing would have us believe. Another major issue in China is the media, which is still tightly controlled. Access to certain websites is blocked and foreign broadcasts are jammed if they are considered threatening to 'national security' or 'political stability' – in other words, anything that goes against the official Communist Party line. However, some foreign broadcasts are now allowed via cable, and as China's contact with the capitalist world increases, there is no reason to doubt that media freedoms will grow.

As well as holding the record as the world's most populous nation, China also has the dubious honour of holding the world record for the most executions carried out per year. In 1999, China executed 1,077 people, although this is thought to be only a fraction of the true figure, given that extra judicial executions are commonplace as are 'disappearances'. As well as a huge number of executions, China still sends to labour camps any outspoken dissidents and those who support proscribed organisation, such as the Falun Gong movement. China's appalling human rights record goes to show that much has to be done before China can be considered a free, democratic nation and therefore in no way a threat to us.

So what can be done by the West to aid China's progress towards democracy and freedom? The answer is simple; wait. China is now a communist state with a market-based, positively capitalist economy. As the two, that is capitalism and communism, are clearly not compatible, one must eventually give way to the other and it is clear that in China's case, it will be communism that gives way to capitalism. This fall of communism is inevitable in China simply because capitalism in China has already too much of a positive influence on China for it to go back to old communism. And, as I outlined in the first chapter of this book, capitalism and communism cannot coexist in the same government: it has to be one or the other; there is no third way. I believe that quasi-democracy will spread throughout China and will, as it did in the USSR, lead to real democracy coming about in the not too distant future (probably in about twenty to thirty years). The future, both economic and political, is looking much brighter for China, for that future is a free, capitalist future.

Conclusions

- Communism is no longer the threat it was to the West during the Cold War, although it still poses a threat, mainly in the form of North Korea.

- Communism is crumbling away before capitalism.

- We are therefore witnessing the reverse domino effect, in that communist countries are falling one after another to capitalism rather than vice versa.

- The few remaining communist countries are gradually becoming more capitalist, but they are still communist.

- Communism in Vietnam is falling for one main reason:

its people have had increased contact with the outside (i.e. capitalist) world.

- Tourism is the main source of this contact.

- Tourism has helped open the Vietnamese economy simply because Hanoi can see how much money can be made out of tourism.

- Hanoi still restricts access to information in an attempt to remain in power, though this will change as Vietnam becomes yet more capitalist.

- When communism falls in Vietnam it is not likely to be sudden nor is Vietnam likely to need much in the way of economic aid.

- The only assistance that Vietnam is likely to require is from independent observers to ensure that its elections are free and democratic.

- By continuing to trade with Vietnam, we are helping to hasten the end of communism there.

- Cuba's current state of economic collapse is largely due to Fidel Castro's refusal to diversify the Cuban economy.

- Cuba's economy began to decline when the USSR fell, taking the $5 billion a year subsidies with it.

- Cuba still retains all the classic hallmarks of a communist state: an interfering, repressive, Gestapo-style state security force, a controlled economy, and an un-free media.

- The Cuban security forces disallow contact between Cubans and foreign visitors, lest the Cubans gain any ideas that are unbecoming in a communist state.

- The Cuban government's style is summed up by the fact that it is an offence, punishable with imprisonment, to insult (or, in other words, disagree with) a Cuban government official.

- The desire to keep its grip on power, not some marvellous revelation, is what has made Havana become ever so slightly more economically free.

- Tourism, which Havana encourages to get the currency it needs to prop itself up with, will leak Western ideas into Cuba, which will help to bring around an end to communism in Cuba.

- There are two likely ways in which communism will fall in Cuba. The first, which would take many years to come about, is for a Berlin Wall-style fall of communism. The second, most likely scenario is for Castro's regime to fall in some kind of coup.

- If the new regime was willing to be democratic, then with our assistance, Cuba could become a free and prosperous nation.

- However, if the new regime was extremist (i.e. hardline communist) we would have the danger of a state intent on the destruction of America, using its new ally's strategic advantage, as the USSR did in 1962.

- If this, the worst-case scenario, were to happen we would have a simple choice: remove the regime by force or face the potentially apocalyptic consequences.

- When it comes to dealing with China, the West should not be scared of China's 'nuclear' status – the figures show that.

- China has made huge steps in the right direction; its free-enterprise reforms have caused living standards across China to go up.

- China's political freedom still lags behind its economic freedom – though as the two are inextricably linked, there can be little doubt that the former will catch up.

- The quasi-democracy at a local level will, chances are, lead to real democracy; as it did in the USSR.

- China is a newly industrialising nation; it is not yet an economic superpower, as Beijing would have us believe.

- Media freedoms are still restricted in China, however, change is on the horizon with recent legalisation of some foreign cable channels.

- China still has a long way to go before it can be considered free and democratic and therefore in no way a threat to us.

- China currently is a capitalist-communist state, things that are incompatible. Therefore one, communism, will give way to the other, capitalism.

- In the not too distant future, the current quasi-democracy in China will become real democracy, something that will herald a new free dawn for China.

Postscript

The main theme of this book, which I hope has been present from the outset, is freedom – the most important right of all. Indeed, it is true to say that without all rights (be it freedom of choice, freedom of speech) freedom is incomplete and that without freedom all other rights are incomplete; it is no coincidence that many 'rights' have the word 'freedom' in their names. I believe that everybody on earth has the right to freedom – especially the right to freedom of opinion and expression. As I said at the beginning of this book, I believe that an opinion is pointless if it is not expressed, but to do this there must be one prerequisite: freedom. There are many people on earth – some in the countries that I have mentioned and some in others – that do not have the opportunity to express their views, which, alongside the removal of the freedom of choice, I find to be the most despicable human rights abuse of all. Indeed, that is the reason for my writing this book: my belief that everybody should have freedom, be it freedom from war, freedom from oppression, freedom of choice or freedom of speech.

This belief, which I believe to be shared by most people, raises the question of what lengths we should go to to preserve and enable people to have this freedom. As I write these lines, we approach the sixtieth anniversary of D-Day, the beginning of Operation Overlord, which freed Europe from Nazi tyranny and gave millions their freedom. The heroic sacrifices made on the Normandy beaches and elsewhere by so many men, most of them not much older than myself, are what has made it possible for me to write this book and indeed for people to have opinions for or against my own. Without their bravery, there can be little doubt that most, if not all, of the world would not have the freedom that we in the West take for granted. The one thing that must be remembered – more importantly, must never be forgotten – is what happened the last time a regime that blatantly took freedom away gained major credence, and the sacrifices that had to be made to save the world from that tyranny and to give people back their freedom. The day that we forget this is the day that we start down the slippery slope that led us to the terrible events of the Second World War. We must always be willing to stand up for and to fight for freedom, for freedom is just as important now as it always will be, as it was at any time in the past.

Select Bibliography and Further Reading

Books

Hayek, F A, *The Road to Serfdom*, Chicago, University of Chicago Press, 1994

Thatcher, Margaret, *Statecraft*, London, HarperCollins, 2003

Thatcher, Margaret, *The Downing Street Years*, London, HarperCollins, 1993

Thatcher, Margaret, *The Path to Power*, London, HarperCollins, 1995

The Hutchinson Paperback Encyclopaedia, Abingdon, Helicon, 1990

Websites and Articles

Winter, Joseph, 'Mugabe outfoxes his critics', BBC News Online, 10 February 2003
<http://news.bbc.co.uk/1/hi/world/africa/2744849.stm>

'A History of Conflict, Israel and the Palestinians', *BBC Online*, 2006
<http://news.bbc.co.uk/1/shared/spl/hi/middle_east/03/v3_ip_t imeline/html/>

AllAfrica Global Media, 2006 <www.allafrica.com>

Consular Information Sheet (Cuba), *US State Department*, 22 May 2006
<http://travel.state.gov/travel/cis_pa_tw/cis/cis_1097.html>

'Iran: Amir Abbas Fakhravar, freelance journalist and prisoner of conscience', *Amnesty International UK*, 13 February 2004
<http://www.amnesty.org.uk/news/press/15199.shtml>

'Iranian WMD and Support of Terrorism, Testimony of Paula De Stutter, US Assistant Secretary for Verification and Compliance', 17 September 2003, *US Department of State*
<http://www.state.gov/t/vci/rls/rm/24494.htm>

Israeli Declaration of Independence
<http://www.yale.edu/lawweb/avalon/mideast/israel.htm>

Israeli Ministry of Foreign Affairs, 2006
<http://www.mfa.gov.il>

'Key Maps, Israel and the Palestinians', *BBC Online*, 2006
<http://news.bbc.co.uk/1/shared/spl/hi/middle_east/03/v3_isra
el_palestinians/maps/html/>

'Margaret Thatcher', Wikipedia, 22 May 2006
<http://en.wikipedia.org/wiki/Margaret_Thatcher> <http://w
ww.palestine-net.com/politics/indep.html>

'Muammar Al Qadhafi: The Consummate Revolutionary Leader of the World Revolution', Revolutionary Committee Movement, Australia, 2006
<http://www.mathaba.net/info/mqadhafi.htm>

'Shukri Ghanem', Wikipedia, 5 June 2006
<http://en.wikipedia.org/wiki/Shukri_Ghanem>

The World Factbook, CIA, 2006
<http://www.cia.gov/cia/publications/factbook/index.html>

Zimbabwean Public Order and Security Act, quoted in Amnesty International's Report 2003
http://web.amnesty.org/report2003/zwe-summary-eng